GIN

Shake, Muddle, Stir

Gin: Shake, Muddle, Stir by Dan Jones

First published in 2016 by Hardie Grant Books, an imprint of Hardie Grant Publishing

Hardie Grant Books (UK)
52–54 Southwark Street
London SE1 1UN

Hardie Grant Books (Australia)
Ground Floor, Building 1
658 Church Street
Melbourne, VIC 3121

hardiegrantbooks.com

British Library Cataloguing-in-Publication Data. A catalogue record for this book is available from the British Library.

ISBN: 978-1-78488-052-1

Publisher: Kate Pollard
Senior Editor: Kajal Mistry
Editorial Assistant: Hannah Roberts
Art Direction: Matt Phare
Illustrator: Daniel Servansky
Copy editor: Kay Delves
Proofreader: Charlotte Coleman-Smith
Indexer: Cathy Heath
Colour Reproduction by p2d

Printed and bound in Italy by Rotolito Lombarda Spa

GIN

Shake, Muddle, Stir

by Dan Jones

ILLUSTRATIONS BY DANIEL SERVANSKY

hardie grant books

CONTENTS

Welcome
to
GIN
Shake, Muddle, Stir

'We are all in the gutter, but some of us are looking at the stars.'

— **Oscar Wilde**, *Lady Windermere's Fan*, Act III

Does anything describe sweet inebriation by the world's finest spirit better than Oscar Wilde's infamous quote? That tickle of citrus, the sharp slap of juniper and the intimate massage of perfectly refined, potent alcohol that leaves many of us rolling around in the gutter: gin builds you up, knocks you down, sends inappropriate selfies to everyone in your contacts and lends you your bus fare home. Perhaps Wilde didn't quite mean gin when he came up with that legendary line (he was more of an absinthe man), but his knowledge of alcohol and its otherworldly effects is undeniable. From its troubled birth on the backstreets in London to its current incarnation as the world's fastest-growing artisanal spirit, gin's salacious past and rosy future is as tasty as a freshly made G & T.

This is *Gin: Shake, Muddle, Stir*. How to mix it, shake it, stir it and – most importantly – how to drink it. A full list of mix-at-home recipes, infusions and syrups, with essential and impressive tools, glassware, marvellous mixers, butt-tingling bitters and the world's very best gins, from British and Scottish classics to international megabrands and fresh, young indie upstarts from the UK to Australia and the States.

Now, let's drink gin.

Dan Jones

THE CRACK OF THE CAPITAL

Let's hear it for gin, that clear, fragrant and undeniably delicious spirit notable for its unique juniper flavour and curious relationship with London, the greatest city on Earth (indisputable, if you've had a few). Not so long ago, gin was the crack of the capital, the unlimited fun-juice guzzled by cackling, wooden-toothed wastrels, hawkers and street walkers, pox-ridden poets and general London lowlifes. In Georgian England, the spirit had a rather dour reputation, leagues away from its refined contemporary incarnation. Gin wasn't the unfashionable grandma's tipple it was perceived to be in the '60s and '70s: it was the demonic broth of the underworld.

A wonderful revolution of government in the late 1600s at the hand of be-wigged Dutchman William of Orange did away with licensing laws, allowing the magic of the distillation process to be available to all, from professional booze-makers to home enthusiasts. This relaxation of the rules meant Londoners did what they do best: got horribly, impossibly drunk. Down-on-their-luck Londoners were tantalised by legendary Dutch spirit Genever, an imported herbal-flavoured liquor drunk by the upper classes. With the real thing out of their reach, they sought to make their own and London dry gin became as available as drinking water, if not more so. With a bit of basic distillation kit, gin could be made in your own home, and was sold across London in grimy taverns, squalid drinking rooms and Mother Clap's infamous Molly House, the city's sauciest drinking venue. Gin gave Londoners a twinkle in their eye, a spring in their step and wrested the city into a binge-drinking crisis.

As gin improved in quality and prices began to rise, the capital-wide obsession with the spirit failed to wane. In the 1800s, glittering gin palaces illuminated the streets – bright, gas-lit venues with huge windows and ornate facades that were in stark contrast to the grime of the street. Inside, Londoners could knock back a gin – known as 'a quick flash of lightning' – cheaper than they could beer, and gin-makers experimented with new flavours and mixers. Gin offered a little pick-me-up to workers on their way home or rocket fuel for those setting out for the night, and gin palaces were just the glamorous venues to drink it in.

Gin and mixers soon evolved into classy long drinks and clever cocktails. Colonial Brits returning from new worlds introduced exotic ingredients (bitter anti-malarial quinine was mixed with gin and sugar in a precursor to the gin and tonic) and the Gimlet, a cocktail of gin and lime juice, was said to ward off scurvy: gin's reputation was on the up. By the mid-1800s the exclusive Garrick Club had mastered a gin punch and cocktail parties replaced the boring formality of Edwardian dinner parties. Forward to the 1930s and Bright Young Things like Stephen Tennant were drinking gin cocktails (in between snifters of 'naughty salt', no doubt).

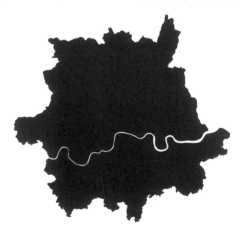

The young Queen Mother's famous love of gin had also marked the spirit out as an unofficial royal concoction yet, by the '60s, gin had a bit of a PR problem. Despite its rough-edged beginnings, it had become associated with the upper classes and acquired uncomfortable colonial affiliations. Quality nose-dived, too, and gin seemed to flatline.

In recent years, craft-edged enterprising indie brands have reanimated the spirit's fortunes, bringing back gin's history of under-the-counter experimentations with modern equipment and fragrant organic botanicals. The UK – the world's leading gin-producing nation – now exports an impressively huge amount of the spirit to new markets that have become obsessed with artisanal versions of the spirit and thoughtfully made mixers. British gin – along with excellent US and European brands – is having a bit of a moment and in the most surprising places: Colombians are crazy for it. London's most famous export (after the Spice Girls, obviously) has come a long way from the back streets of its most squalid neighbourhoods, but it still retains that quick flash of lightning.

GIN: THE SCIENCE BIT

Are you sitting down? This is important. The thing with gin is it can be made from any old 'neutral' spirit – alcohol that has its beginning as grain, barley, maze or even molasses – anything, really. The thing that turns it into the magical giggle-juice of ye olde back alleys of London town is the clever

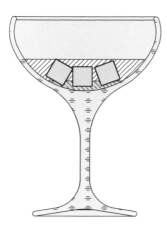

combination of botanicals – from coriander, angelica and orange peel to lemon peel, cardamom, cinnamon, cubeb pepper and nutmeg – with juniper berries in the lead. Most gin producers keep their list of ingredients closely guarded, but all gins include juniper as a must-have. And... that's it. Simple, right? This type of spirit is know as Compound Gin and isn't thought of as highly as other methods, but it can still produce some otherworldly, flavoursome drinks.

London Gin, also known as London Dry Gin, is what most of us mix in our G & Ts. The name is legally defined – it must be 70 per cent ABV (alcohol by volume) with absolutely no fake ingredients and, after the distillation process, no added flavourings or colourings – just a tiny amount of sugar, making it very dry. It can also be made anywhere in the world. The base spirit is diluted with pure water, then mixed with botanicals (combined in whole, in clever little infusion bags, or on a tray above the liquid) and added to a copper still. Then it's heated up to release the delicious botanical and essential oils. The liquid evaporates and is redistilled to capture the magical flavourings. The gin can be distilled in two main ways: column-distilled and pot-stilled. Perhaps the most popular are pot-still gins – the sexy, curvaceous copper pots are given female nicknames, with vintage ones held in high regard. Distilled Gin follows the same method as London Gin, except flavourings can be added after distillation, often in infusion bags, to give a softer, mellow taste.

The World's Best Gins and Tonics

**TRIED AND TESTED, MIXED AND SIPPED, SPILT
AND MOPPED UP: THESE ARE THE WORLD'S VERY
BEST GINS AND TONICS, FROM STEADFAST
MEGABRANDS TO YOUNG INDIE UPSTARTS**

THE WORLD'S BEST GINS

FOR VICTORIAN GUTTERSNIPES

HAYMAN'S 1850 RESERVE

The Hayman family have been in the British gin business since 1863. Christopher Hayman is a true gin expert and the small brand is powered by a deep love of the spirit, a catalogue of secret recipes and Chris's son James and daughter Miranda. Hayman's Reserve harks back to the glittering gin palaces of old, reanimating the style of the spirit as it was in 1850. Subtle and smooth, Hayman's classic gin recipe is aged in wood for a soft, mellow flavour with notes of juniper and coriander (cilantro), a little pepper and a touch of spice.

FOR FRUITY SCOTTISH HERMITS

CAORUNN

To deepest, darkest Scotland and the Balmenach Distillery in Speyside, which turns its hand to a rowan-berry-infused gin called Caorunn (pronounced ka-roon). Lively, fruity flavours and a dry, crisp quality make this small batch nothing short of delicious. Perfectly balanced notes of heather, apple and dandelion make Caorunn a unique herbal experience and subtle enough either to sip or mix with a pared-down tonic.

FOR UPSCALE CITRUS-LOVERS

TANQUERAY NO. TEN

Although Tanqueray is a flagship gin megabrand, exporting internationally in impressive quantities, it still creates premium small batch quantities distilled in its legendary pot number 10. Using vintage equipment isn't essential towards creating a delicious gin, but it goes a long way in preserving the art of artisanal gin-making, and the age-old pot distillation process means only small quantities are produced. Tanqueray No. Ten is a classic London dry gin, incredibly fragrant and floral and packed with zingy citrus. Nice work, Tanqueray.

FOR BATHTIME DRINKERS

BATHTUB GIN

In the dry days of prohibition, American gin-lovers would make illicit concoctions in their bathtubs – harsh enough to strip the enamel – and drink them until their eyes glazed over. Inspired by this loving, obsessive method, US-made Bathtub Gin is created in tiny batches using a copper pot still and is packed with juniper and orange, coriander (cilantro), cardamom, cloves and cinnamon. Winner of the World's Best Compound Gin at the 2015 World Gin Awards, booze brand Professor Cornelius Ampleforth should feel rather proud. This is a mind-blowingly tasty gin, strong and confident with subtle, well-balanced flavours and a soft, creamy feel, which is leagues away from its bathtub beginnings.

FOR TEA-TOTALLERS

BEEFEATER 24

Tea with a drop of gin? It may sound like the ultimate afternoon pick-me-up with a slice of Victoria sponge, but it is arguably the inspiration behind the fragrant Beefeater 24. Created in the heart of London, the well-known gin brand took 18 months to perfect a recipe that includes Japanese sencha tea and Chinese green tea. Its complex botanicals – from Seville orange peel, grapefruit and lemon peel, to juniper, coriander seed, liquorice, angelica root, almond and orris root – are steeped for a full 24 hours, hence the name. Aromatic in the extreme with a smooth finish.

FOR CUCUMBER CONNOISSEURS

HENDRICK'S

The cucumber-powered superstar of contemporary gins, Hendrick's is the extremely small batch, pot-still distilled and blended Scottish juniper gin with big pretensions. Small batch gin is usually made approximately 1,000 litres at a time; Hendrick's plump for just half that – that's 500 litres – using two vintage stills, which means the brand's gin-tasters have greater control over the flavour of each pot. Heavy on the cucumber, Hendrick's has discovered the aromatic vegetable's perfect flavourmate: the rose (or Bulgarian Rosa Damascena, to be exact).

FOR THE SUPER FRESH

MARTIN MILLER'S

Martin Miller's super-fresh gin is a real labour of love. Its unique recipe of botanicals, a curvy vintage pot-still named Angela and geeky dual process (where the earthier botanical ingredients are distilled separately from the lighter, citrus notes) mean Miller's gin has an incredible depth of flavour with each element able to shine through. Miller adds Tuscan juniper, cassia bark, angelica, Florentine orris, coriander (cilantro), Seville citrus peel, nutmeg, cinnamon and liquorice root to the mix with pure Icelandic spring water. Genuinely one of the world's very best gins. Cheers, Martin.

FOR MANIC GERMANICS

MONKEY 47

This award-winning little German number from the legendary Black Forest has it all, not least a toe-curling, eye-popping and mouth-caving strength at 47 per cent proof. Monkey 47 is a complex, woody gin with a fruity, spicy, peppery and herby finish and a cranberry kick for good measure; taking inspiration from classical British gin, Indian influences and the fairytale woods of the Black Forest. There are 47 ingredients, in fact, but this monkey is perfectly balanced, using locally sourced spring water for a fresh touch. Monkey magic.

FOR NON-GIN GIN DRINKERS

BLOOM

Bloom is a gin in disguise. Unapologetically
floral – packed with honeysuckle, Chinese
pomelo (a subtly sweet grapefruit-like citrus
fruit) and French chamomile – Bloom is scant on
the juniper, lending it a fresher, more upbeat
taste than traditional London dry gin. Master
Distiller Joanne Moore (the only known female
master distiller in the world) was inspired by the
aroma of English country gardens and
wildflower meadows, Bloom is a bit of a show-off
on the award circuit – it has scooped up more
than 15 gongs in recent times, including the
prestigious Platinum Medal at the World Spirits
Competition in 2010.

FOR TIPSY CHASERS

WILLIAMS CHASE

Will Chase grew up on a farm in England, amongst trailers of fresh,
fragrant barley, cider fruit and earthy planting potatoes, and soon
discovered he had a head for business and a bod for eating the world's best
chips. Using his own potatoes, Will's crisp brand, Tyrrells (named after the
family farm), is world-famous and his eponymous award-winning gin is
100 per cent stunning. In making Williams Chase gin, Will swapped his
much-loved rare potatoes for apples, distilling his own biodynamic apple

cider into vodka, and then redistilling it into gin – a hugely lengthy process, but one that produces a unique, fragrant and fresh spirit. There are notes of spice and citrus, cinnamon and nutmeg with a traditional juniper aroma, and it's fantastic in a G & T. So, we can thank Will for bringing two magical things into the world: crisps and gin. The man deserves a medal.

FOR OUTCASTS AND ODDBALLS

BUTLER'S LEMONGRASS & CARDAMOM

To Hackney Wick, now – the East London industrial neighbourhood whose grimy countenance is in sharp contrast to its shiny neighbour, the Olympic Park. It's a place for outcasts and oddballs and the perfect base for Butler's Gin, an artisan spirit with a little East End swagger. Inspired by a ye olde Victorian recipe, Butler's use a 20-litre infusion jar containing fresh lemongrass, cardamom, coriander (cilantro), cloves, cinnamon, star anise, fennel, lemon and lime – tied up in infusion bags – and hand bottle their strongly perfumed (yet delicately flavoured) spirit after 18 hours. Butler's has a pale yellow-green tone and is best served chilled, with cucumber. A refined concoction from the wrong side of the tracks.

FOR INKED-UP DRINKERS

FIFTY EIGHT

Mark Marmont's Fifty Eight is distilled just once in ridiculously tiny batches, hand-labelled and wonkily wax sealed, with artwork by lauded London tattoo artist Mo Coppoletta. The makers add grain spirit to an alembic copper still with nine pungent botanicals including juniper, coriander (cilantro), lemon, pink grapefruit, vanilla, orris root, cubeb pepper, bergamot and angelica. The result is a verdant, fresh spirit with a little citrus, pepper and pine nuts, a touch of sweetness and a big meaty slap of juniper at the end. Fifty Eight makes a stunning G & T, a rich Negroni and a delicate Martini.

FOR DRUNKEN KOALA-LOVERS

FOUR PILLARS

To Australia, now, and the picturesque Yarra Valley in Victoria where the tiny Four Pillars distillery creates its excellent barrel-aged gin amongst communities of kookaburras and koalas (possibly). Four Pillars' pot still, named Wilma, uses triple-filtered Yarra Valley water and a curious recipe of botanicals – local, exotic and traditional – and the Four Pillars team employ real patience in letting their bright, sparky gin rest in French oak barrels for three to six months. Cinnamon, cardamom and a juicy citrus give way to a fresh juniper hit with star anise and lavender. A delightful, considered concoction that's delicious in a G & T.

FOR DRINKERS AND DOG-LOVERS

MOONSHINE KID'S DOG'S NOSE

Meet Matt Whiley, the Moonshine Kid, a British cocktail obsessive and founding member of Fluid Movement, the creatives behind a range of contemporary cocktail bars. His Dog's Nose Gin is made right at the very heart of the spirit's London birthplace, and is cold-distilled under vacuum, with Chinook and Columbus hops and an edit of classic botanicals. Coriander and fresh lemon blend with juniper and borage to give a hoppy, creamy feel, plus a little spice for good measure. It's a real mixer's spirit and is delicious and complex in cocktails.

FOR WINOS WITH WISDOM

NO. 209

Meet No. 209, the 209th distillery to be registered in the United States, one of the world's finest small batch, handcrafted spirit-makers and, perhaps, the only Kosher-for-Passover gin creator in the world. Distilled four times, the clever complexity of No. 209's citrus and spice taste comes from bergamot orange, lemon peel, cardamom pods, cassia bark, angelica root and coriander seeds, along with a powerful punch of juniper. Winemakers by trade, 209 also age gin in used wine barrels, and their No. 209 Cabernet

Sauvignon Barrel Reserve Gin has a magical amber hue. With real care and attention, 209 make a premium, masterful and contemporary gin.

FOR THOSE LOST IN AUSTEN

BATH GIN

With Jane Austen winking out from its label, Bath Gin is keen to underline its literary pretensions and affiliation with Bath, the English UNESCO World Heritage city, but it's the tasty botanicals that excite: cassia bark, lemon peel, smoky burnt orange peel, cubeb berry, liquorice, cardamom, angelica root and juniper. Created by the Canary Gin Bar in Bath, England – in small batch numbered bottles – this delightful gin's use of wormwood and kaffir lime leaf is inspired, creating a considered, premium gin that is worthy of Jane Austen herself. She, no doubt, would have loved a little pick-me-up between chapters.

FOR SECRET PROHIBITION SIPPERS

FEW AMERICAN GIN

This mind-blowing American gin from the Few craft distillery in Evanston, Illinois (the birthplace of Prohibition), cheekily takes its name from the initials of Frances Elizabeth Willard, a key figure in the Temperance Movement. Unlike most gins, this one begins life as a white whiskey – an aged bourbon – and this gives it a completely unique character. With a lemon zest and juniper aroma, Few gives way to a sweet vanilla finish with a clean, pure freshness. Few Spirits was the first distillery within the city limits since Prohibition, and the company's diligent approach to creating alcohol is like a popped cork – this distillery is all about creativity and humour. Case in point: their 2015 limited edition Breakfast Gin powered with Earl Grey.

THE WORLD'S BEST TONIC WATERS

Gin is nothing without its partner in crime, tonic water, and gin and gourmet mixers are the perfect pairing. Tried and tested, here are world's three finest tonics for your sipping pleasure

FEVER-TREE

The big success story. Award-winning Fever-Tree is the little British brand that took on the big boys and carved a place for itself in the world's finest restaurants, hotels, bars – and bodega shelves. It is made from botanical oils, spring water and the highest quality quinine from the 'fever trees' of the eastern Congo – the ingredient that gives tonic water its slightly bitter edge. With fresh green ginger, elderflowers and natural cane sugar, Fever-Tree is a wonderfully considered tonic – the antithesis of mass-produced megabrands. It brings a fresh, almost handcrafted, kick to a G & T. Pair it with subtle spirits – artisanal gins packed with heavy juniper notes can become a little overpowering when mixed with a little beauty like this. A drink in its own right.

FENTIMANS

Fentimans is the 100-year-old artisanal drinks maker that creates botanically brewed and hands-down delicious mixers. The brand's light and herbal tonic waters are perfect, the latter blended with hyssop and myrtle. But it's their regular tonic water, powered with lemongrass, that packs a punch. In the early 1900s, Fentimans sold their beverages (mainly ginger beer) door-to-door in stone jars emblazoned with the company mascot – a dog called Fearless. These days, things are a little different. Fentimans is an international brand with an impressive range of drinks and mixers, alcoholic drinks and one very tasty regular tonic water.

SCHWEPPES

Schweppes is the world's most popular tonic – with a watertight history of getting it right – so it's easy to forget how perfect it is. Craft mixers are creating real excitement in bar-world, but Schweppes tonic water, with its wonderfully prickly fizz and well-balanced bitter–sweet ratio is completely unique. It's generally considered the barman's favourite, letting the complex qualities of premium gin sing out loud and proud. So, while the home mixer might fall for brands like Fever-Tree and Fentimans, Schweppes is nothing to be sniffed at.

Essential Gin Gadgetry

DON'T KNOW YOUR HAWTHORNE STRAINER FROM YOUR JIGGER? THE RIGHT GADGETS ELEVATE A GIN COCKTAIL FROM NICE AND TASTY TO BRAIN-NUMBINGLY EXCELLENT

IMPRESSIVE TOOLS

Invest in your own at-home gin palace with a range of impressive cocktail-making tools. Start off simple: a shaker, jigger, blender, strainer, and an ice bucket. Here's what you'll need to keep it minimal:

JIGGER

A toolbox essential. The jigger is the standard measure for spirits and liqueurs and is available in many different sizes. Heavy metallic jiggers look the part, but plastic or glass versions also do the job. If you don't have a jigger or single shot glass as a stand-in, use an egg cup – at least then your ratios will be right, even if your shots might be a little over-generous – failing that, cross your fingers and free-pour your drinks.

MIXING GLASS

A simple, sturdy straight-sided glass (also known as the Boston) – or a straight-sided pint glass that tapers out – for cocktails that need stirring with a bar spoon rather than shaking or to allow for extra volume when attached to the can of your shaker (to make two or more drinks at a time). The two halves are locked together and you shake until the drink is chilled, then a hawthorne strainer can be used to strain the drink into a fresh glass.

SHAKER

Sometimes known as the Boston Shaker, it's the home mixer's silver bullet. This is your single most important piece of kit as very few cocktails are possible without one. The classic metallic model has three main parts: a base, known as the 'can' (a tall, tumbler shape that tapers out), a tight-fitting funnel top with built-in strainer, onto which a small cap fits (which can also be used as a jigger). It's brilliantly straightforward and, like all the finest tools, it pays to keep it scrupulously clean. If you can't get your hands on one consider a large glass jar with a lid and waterproof seal.

BLENDER

Essential for fruity little numbers. Unless you're using a NutriBullet, most domestic blenders find ice a little difficult, so it's best to use crushed ice in blender cocktails, rather than cubes or rocks. Add your ingredients first, then the ice, and start off on a slow speed before turning it up to max. No need to strain. Once the consistency is super-smooth, pour into a glass and serve.

HAWTHORNE STRAINER

The showy-looking strainer, trimmed with a spring, comes in handy when your shaker's built-in version isn't up to the job. Place on a glass and pour the cocktail through it or hold up against the cocktail can or mixing glass and pour from a height. Wash immediately after use, especially if you're straining a cream-based cocktail. A fine tea strainer does the job brilliantly, but the classic hawthorne really looks the part.

JUICER

For extracting the pure juice from fruit or ginger, etc – rather than adding the pith, skin, seeds and fibres as with a smoothie – you'll need a juicer. It's an investment, sure, but you'll end up with the next level in gin cocktails, and think of all the green juice #cleaneating Instagram opportunities.

CHOPPING BOARD AND KNIFE

Simple, but essential. Keep the board clean, the knife super sharp and practise your peeling skills: the aim is to avoid as much white pith as possible, leaving just the peel that is studded with aromatic oils.

CITRUS SQUEEZER

A clever and pleasingly simple invention: the citrus squeezer is a hand press for all 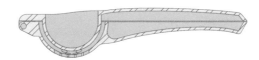 your citrus fruits. Chop the fruit in half, place in the squeezer, then press with all your might as the juice runs out and the pips and pith stay behind. Always use fresh citrus juices. If you don't have a lemon squeezer, use your hands to squeeze the juice through your fingers, catching the pips as you go.

ICE BUCKET

The centrepiece of your home bar; it can be simple, functional and slightly retro or the full plastic pineapple. An insulated ice bucket means your ice cubes will keep their shape for longer, and a good set of tongs adds a touch of class.

UPSCALE EXTRAS

ICE PICK

Buy bags of filtered, crushed ice or cubes (and always buy double or triple the amount you think you'll need) or attack your own home-made ice block with an ice pick. Boil water, let it cool slightly and pour into an old plastic ice-cream container. Freeze solid, turn out onto a clean tea towel (dish towel), and then attack as needed with a firm grip. The ice will go everywhere, but bear with it. Keep the rocks large and jagged for drinks like the New Fashioned (page 118).

MUDDLER

A short, usually wooden baton used to mash and muddle fruit, herbs, ice and sugar in the glass, bruising and bashing up your ingredients to release their natural oils and flavours. Think of it as a pestle and mortar for your drink. If you don't have a muddler, use a flat-ended rolling pin (with caution!).

COCKTAIL STICK

For spearing cherries, citrus peel, fruit slices, olives, onion slivers, pickles. Sausages, even.

SWIZZLE STICK

More than just cocktail furniture, the swizzle allows the drinker to navigate their own drink, stirring as they go. Great for drinks packed with fresh fruit and garnishes or for nervous partygoers who need something to fiddle with.

CANELE OR JULIENNE KNIFE

A fancy bit of kit: the canele knife has a V-shaped groove for cutting citrus peel spirals, carving melons and probably many other crafty uses.

NOVELTY STRAWS, PARASOLS AND PLASTIC MONKEYS

Tricky. Creating amazing cocktails means that they should taste and look otherworldly just as they are. That's without parasols, plastic monkeys, flashing LED ice cubes and novelty straws you can wear as glasses. That said, there's something more than a little pleasing about adding the odd frill to your drink. Make sure straws are part of your home bar toolkit – stripy red and white paper ones are pretty eye-catching – and the odd plastic monkey never hurt anyone. Maybe save your penis straws for extra special occasions like 80th birthday parties.

BAR SPOON

The classic bar spoon has a long, twisted handle, a flat end and a teardrop-shaped spoon used for stirring and measuring out ingredients. It's not essential, but looks pretty cool.

A Guide to Glasses

**STEER AWAY FROM USING ORDINARY
GLASSWARE TO SERVE DRINKS. THE HOME
MIXER SHOULD TAKE A LITTLE PRIDE IN WHAT
THEY PRESENT AND INVEST IN SOME UPSCALE
COUPES, TUMBLERS AND HIGHBALLS**

COUPE

The short, trumpet-shaped glass perfect for Champagne and sparkling wines and a respectable martini glass alternative. (**Fig. 1**)

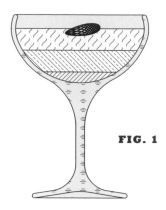

FIG. 1

MARTINI

Cocktail culture's most iconic glass: the refined stem and cone-shaped glass flares out to create a large, shallow recess. Somehow loses its ability not to slosh out its contents as the evening wears on. (**Fig. 2**)

MOSCOW MULE MUG

The iconic copper mug, traditionally used for a Moscow Mule or Mojito, forms a refreshing-looking, frosty condensation when packed with ice.

FIG. 2

CHAMPAGNE FLUTE

The flute-shaped glass used for Champagne cocktails, Bellinis and Mimosas. (**Fig. 3, overleaf**)

COLLINS GLASS

The skinny, usually straight-sided version of the Highball. (**Fig. 4**)

HIGHBALL

Ostensibly a tall glass, with a thick and sturdy bottom, that holds 225–350 ml (8–12 oz) perfectly mixed booze. (**Fig. 5**)

TUMBLER

The short, straight-sided glass perfect for short or single shot drinks. Like most things, best to pick one with a heavy bottom. (**Fig. 6**)

BOSTON GLASS

The twin brother of the straight-sided pint glass, swapped at birth. Great for mixing in or for using locked into the can of your shaker. (**Fig. 7**)

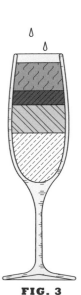

FIG. 3

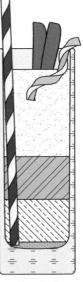

FIG. 4

FIG. 5

TIKI MUG

The tiki mug was born in mid-twentieth century American tiki bars and attributed to Don the Beachcomber, the founding father of tiki culture. It's a tall, wonky-looking ceramic mug with a face like an Easter Island statue.

JAM JAR

There are no hard-and-fast rules for how you serve your drinks – or rather what you serve them in. You can use any number of alternatives – jam jars, tea cups, sciencey test tubes and beakers, Russian tea glasses, shoes – to get your guests beyond the pale. (**Fig 8**)

SHOT GLASS

Short and simple. Pour, drink, slam down. Done. Also doubles as a jigger.

FIG. 6

FIG. 7

FIG. 8

Tricks of the Trade

IT'S NOT WHAT YOU HAVE, IT'S WHAT YOU DO WITH IT. THERE'S MORE TO MAKING A GIN COCKTAIL THAN GRABBING A SHAKER AND FURIOUSLY BASHING ONE OUT. LIKE ALL THE BEST THINGS, THERE'S AN ART TO IT

HOW TO DO IT

HOW TO SHAKE

There's a war going on in cocktail land. How long exactly to shake the perfect concoction? No one can agree. Some say 15 seconds of brisk shaking, others say less. This book is going out on a limb and settles on a short and sharp 7 seconds. Any longer could dilute the drink a little too much, affecting potency. Otherwise, there should be no bottle flipping or sparkler lighting, although a little lemon and lime juggling wouldn't go amiss.

HOW TO STIR

Whip out your bar spoon, and your mixing glass, and stir drinks gently and deftly with ice to chill the concoction. When condensation forms on the outside of the glass, it's ready to go.

HOW TO CHILL

If you have room, clear a shelf in your freezer and keep your cocktail glasses on ice, or pack them full of cubes to throw away when the glass is chilled.

POTENCY

All cocktails are potent, but some are more potent than others. Each drink should seek to achieve a perfect balance of flavours and can attempt differing levels of intensity, but shouldn't get you drunk – at least not on its own. Perfect measurements really matter.

THE LOOK

Fresh garnishes, squeaky clean glasses, clear, purified ice and a perfect balance of colours and visible textures are essential.

AROMATICS

Your drink should smell really, really great – not just taste good. Bitters, fresh juices and citrus peels packed with fragrant oils help achieve this.

HOW TO PUT TOGETHER YOUR BACK BAR

Apart from a collection of the world's best gins – from Hendrick's to Tanqueray – and your own home-made infusions, create a back bar with a mix of strong, clean and classic spirits, the odd special buy, and a few rarities. You don't need to stock up on fine vintage spirits for cocktails – their subtler qualities are lost in the mixing – but you do need to invest in something of quality.

GIN

Mother's ruin, hell broth, giggle-juice, the quick flash of lightning... Make sure your gin is premium enough for sipping and remember to mix the subtler spirits with mixers and save the flavourful ones for cocktails that let the botanicals sing out – like a dry Martini or a Gin Old Fashioned. The perfect back bar would have one small batch, handcrafted premium gin and a couple of upscale contenders for mixing.

WHISKEY

Pick a sturdy, deep-tasting bourbon rather than an aged malt. Monkey Shoulder, Knob Creek and Bulleit Bourbon are all strong contenders.

VERMOUTH

The fortified wine packed with botanicals, in sweet or dry versions. Get both and keep them refrigerated after opening.

TEQUILA

The agave-based brain melter. Unaged (or aged for no more than 60 days in steel containers), silver (*blanco*) tequila is an

essential part of your back bar. Gold tequila is sweet and smooth, coloured and flavoured with caramel; *reposado* ('rested') tequila, aged in wood-lined tanks or barrels, brings a smoky undertone to your mixes.

VODKA

Stolichnaya, Smirnoff and Absolut are all reliable brands, while the more expensive Crystal Head vodka – encased in a skull-shaped bottle – certainly looks the part.

RUM

Rum is the liquor sailors drink to ward off scurvy. Cheap rum, that is. Invest a little in an upscale number like Zacapa or Brugal Añejo and you'll feel less *Pirates of the Caribbean* and more Donald Trump's yacht. Light rum, milder in flavour, is easier to mix.

CAMPARI AND APEROL

Sharp, ruby red bitters that pep up cocktails and form the basis of the Negroni and Americano. They are really quite life-changing mixed with soda water and chilled sparkling wine.

CASSIS

Invest in a good-quality crème de cassis or crème de mûre: dark berry-flavoured liqueurs for Kirs, Kir Royales and more besides – they're the perfect sweetener in pared-down gin recipes. Mix a drop of cassis into a G & T to give it a sweet berry kick.

TRIPLE SEC AND ORANGE LIQUEUR

A back bar essential, triple sec (or a high-quality orange liqueur like Cointreau) is made from the dried peel of sweet and bitter oranges and has a deep, rich flavour that is the perfect element for many cocktails.

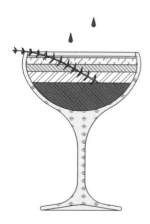

SYRUP

A cocktail essential. Simple syrup – aka gomme or sugar syrup – is liquid sugar and, mixed part-for-part with sharp citrus juices, brings a delightfully sweet-sour note to a recipe. Buy a premium version of simple syrup (Monin is a good, decent brand) or make your own (page 45). Agave syrup is a naturally occurring syrup that is available in raw, light and amber – light is best for most cocktails as it has a clean, simple taste.

BITTERS

Angostura bitters (Venezuelan-by-way-of-Trinidad-and-Tobago aromatics) are an essential element of the back bar. Said to be a cure for hiccups, the part-herbal, part-alcoholic tinctures are highly aromatic, giving cocktails a depth of taste and colouring white spirits a subtle sunrise pink. Bitters and cordial producers Fee Brothers (est. 1863) is another good brand to start with: their whisky

barrel-aged bitters with rhubarb and plum flavours are particularly mouth-caving.

PREMIUM TONIC WATER

Gin's turnaround from an unpopular, rather unfashionable spirit to the world's fastest-growing liquor industry, dominated by UK independent brands, is remarkable. Premium tonic water, powered by brands like Fever-Tree and Fentimans, has helped drag gin into the spotlight. Fever-Tree is the international indie brand that has reminded gin lovers of an important boozy fact: tonic is supposed to taste wonderful. For years, mass market commercial tonic water seemed a necessary evil until Fever-Tree launched in 2005, and was soon discovered by El Bulli chef Ferran Adrià who used it in a liquid nitrogen-cooled granita and helped kick-start a gin renaissance (gin-aissance?) in Spain, across Europe and beyond. Fentimans is the more than 100-year-old drinks producer who knows more than a thing or two about what makes the perfect mixer. Check out the World's Best Tonic Waters on page 22.

MIXERS

They say no one uses cola as a mixer any more. No one (although you're permitted a splash in a Long Island Iced Tea). But make sure you have a ginger beer or ale, chilled sparkling water or soda, prosecco, cava or Champagne and freshly squeezed citrus juices, premium cloudy lemonade, cranberry juice, elderflower cordial, coconut water and – always – a truckload of ice.

BARELY LEGAL

In 1920s prohibition New York you might have needed a bathtub, new fangled distillation equipment and a cast-iron liver to make your own gin. These days, it's a far more civilised affair. Making your own gin relies on the fact that gin and vodka are practically twins with a fermentation and distillation process that is startlingly similar. If vodka is a pared-down, clean and clear drink with little or no taste, homemade gin is, basically, vodka infused with aromatic herbs, spices and botanicals. Juniper berries are – for gin purists – an essential ingredient, but this method of infusing vodka and turning it into mother's ruin leaves all the creativity up to you.

HOMEMADE GIN

Juniper is the deep, dark core flavour of gin. The berries (actually a sort of squishy seed cone) lend the spirit its herbal flavour. Cinnamon and cardamom pods – split open so the seeds can fall out – lend an exotic note. Although citrus peel aroma is particularly uplifting, its flavour is notoriously bitter. Make sure you've trimmed away all the white pith. Liquorice root should add a little sweetness. Lime or bay leaves add a fresh, verdant zing.

INGREDIENTS

500 ml (17 fl oz) good vodka (not the harsh, paint-stripper stuff)

large pinch of juniper berries

pinch of cardamom pods

1 liquorice root stick

1 cinnamon stick

orange, lemon and lime peel (100% pith-free)

1–2 lime or bay leaves

EQUIPMENT sterilised airtight bottle, strainer

METHOD Steep the ingredients in the vodka and place your sterilised , sealed bottle in a dark, cool place for at least 3 days – or longer if you want a stronger taste. Strain the ingredients from the liquid and serve.

Infusions, Syrups, Sours and Brines

**SUPERCHARGE A BASIC
(BUT GOOD-QUALITY) GIN WITH YOUR OWN
INFUSIONS OR CREATE A SIMMERED-DOWN
REDUCTION TO ADD A POWER-PUNCH
OF FLAVOUR**

INFUSIONS

SLOE & STAR ANISE GIN

Prick a handful of fresh, ripe sloe berries and add these to 500 ml (17 oz) of gin along with a single star anise pod, bashed into manageable pieces, and 1 teaspoon of brown sugar. Let it steep for at least 3 days in a cool, dark place before straining and serving. Store for up to 6 weeks in the fridge in the original bottle. Best in a Slow Gin & Tempranillo Negroni (page 96).

BAY LEAF GIN

Use 2–3 fresh bay leaves per 500 ml (17 oz) of gin. Let it steep for at least 3 days in a cool, dark place before straining and serving. Store for up to 6 weeks in the fridge in the original bottle.

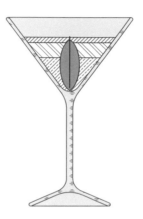

Otherworldly in a Bay Leaf & Green Tea Martini (page 100).

GINGER GIN

This fiery infusion creates a rather spicy note. Add a thumb-sized, peeled piece of fresh ginger to 500 ml (17 oz) of gin. Let it steep for at least 3 days in a cool, dark place before straining and removing the ginger. Store for up to 6 weeks in the fridge in the original bottle.

SYRUPS AND REDUCTIONS

The sweet stuff. Taking the edge off sour citrus flavours and softening the taste of bitter spirits, a dash of sugar syrup can transform a drink, turning the toughest liquor into soda pop. Flavoured, syrup adds a level of complexity a fresh ingredient just can't achieve. And it's very nearly foolproof to make. Start with this Simple Syrup recipe, graduate to the flavoured infusions and then begin to create your own. You could always buy them ready-made, but it's so simple, you really don't need to.

It's not essential to use unrefined sugar, but it's tastier, chemical-free and lends a wobbly irregularity to proceedings that could only be handmade.

TEMPRANILLO REDUCTION

Makes enough dashes for approximately 15 drinks

INGREDIENTS

200 ml (7 oz) Tempranillo wine

pinch of crushed star anise

100 g (3½ oz) dark brown sugar

1 tablespoon corn syrup or golden syrup (optional)

EQUIPMENT Non-stick saucepan, wooden spoon, 200 ml (7 oz) kilner jar or glass bottle with stopper and a funnel

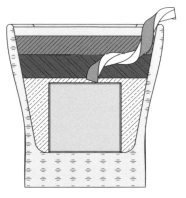

METHOD Simmer the wine and star anise in a non-stick saucepan and gently add the sugar. Turn down the heat and stir constantly with a wooden spoon for 3–5 minutes, until all the sugar is dissolved and the mixture has reduced by approximately one-third. Turn off the heat and leave to cool for 20–30 minutes for the flavours to infuse. While still runny, decant into a sterilised kilner jar or funnel into a sterilised glass bottle with a stopper. Adding a spoonful of corn syrup to the cooled mixture now will help keep the reduction smooth. Store in the fridge for up to 6 weeks.

SIMPLE SYRUP

Makes enough dashes for
approximately 15 drinks

INGREDIENTS

200 ml (7 oz) water

100 g (3½ oz) unrefined demerara,
cane or granulated (raw) sugar

1 tablespoon corn syrup or golden syrup
(optional)

EQUIPMENT Non-stick saucepan,
wooden spoon, 200 ml (7 oz) kilner jar
or glass bottle with stopper and a funnel

METHOD Boil the water in a
non-stick saucepan and gently add the
sugar. Turn down the heat and stir
constantly with a wooden spoon for
3–5 minutes, until all the sugar is
dissolved and the syrup is clear. »

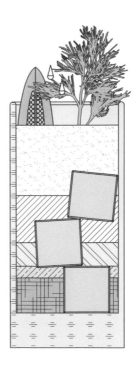

Turn off the heat and leave to cool. While still runny, pour into a sterilised kilner jar or funnel into a sterilised glass bottle with a stopper. Adding a spoonful of corn syrup to the cooled mixture now will help keep the syrup smooth. Store in the fridge for up to 6 weeks.

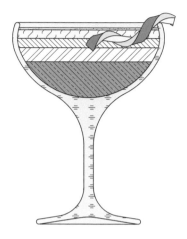

RHUBARB, GINGER & STAR ANISE SYRUP

Makes enough dashes for approximately 15 drinks

INGREDIENTS

200 ml (7 oz) water

100 g (3½ oz) unrefined demerara, cane or granulated (raw) sugar

2 rhubarb stalks, cut into chunks

1 tablespoon grated fresh ginger

1 star anise, slightly crushed

dash of lemon juice, freshly squeezed

1 tablespoon corn syrup or golden syrup (optional)

EQUIPMENT Non-stick saucepan, wooden spoon, cheesecloth, heatproof bowl, 200 ml (7 oz) kilner jar or glass bottle with stopper and a funnel

METHOD Boil the water in a non-stick saucepan and gently add the sugar, rhubarb, ginger, star anise and lemon juice. Turn down the heat and stir constantly with a wooden spoon for 3–5 minutes, until all the sugar is dissolved. Turn off the heat and leave to cool for 20–30 minutes. While still runny, pass through a cheesecloth-lined strainer into a heatproof bowl, then decant into a sterilised kilner jar or funnel into a sterilised glass bottle with stopper. Adding a spoonful of corn syrup now will help keep the mixture smooth. Store in the fridge for up to 6 weeks.

SPICED BROWN SUGAR SYRUP

Makes enough dashes for approximately 15 drinks

INGREDIENTS

200 ml (7 oz) water

100 g (31/2 oz) unrefined dark brown sugar

1 tablespoon grated fresh ginger

1 tablespoon corn syrup or golden syrup (optional)

EQUIPMENT Non-stick saucepan, wooden spoon, cheesecloth, heatproof bowl, 200 ml (7 oz) kilner jar or glass bottle with stopper and a funnel

METHOD Boil the water in a non-stick saucepan and gently add the sugar and ginger. Turn down the heat and stir constantly with a wooden spoon for 3–5 minutes, until all the sugar is dissolved. Turn off the heat and »

leave to cool for 20–30 minutes for the flavours to infuse. While still runny, pass through a cheesecloth-lined strainer into a heatproof bowl, then decant into a sterilised kilner jar or funnel into a sterilised glass bottle with a stopper. Adding a spoonful of corn syrup to the cooled mixture now will help keep the syrup smooth. Store in the fridge for up to 6 weeks.

CHERRY & THYME SYRUP

Makes enough dashes for approximately 15 drinks

INGREDIENTS

200 ml (7 oz) water

100 g (3½ oz) unrefined demerara, cane or granulated (raw) sugar

handful of ripe, squishy cherries, stoned

large sprig of fresh thyme

1 tablespoon corn syrup or golden syrup (optional)

EQUIPMENT Non-stick saucepan, wooden spoon, 200 ml (7 oz) kilner jar or glass bottle with stopper and a funnel

METHOD Boil the water in a non-stick saucepan and gently add the sugar, cherries and thyme. Turn down the heat and stir constantly for 3–5 minutes, until all the sugar is dissolved. Turn off the heat and leave to cool. While still runny, pour into a sterilised kilner jar or funnel into a sterilised glass bottle with stopper. Adding a spoonful of corn syrup to the cooled mixture will help keep the syrup smooth. Store in the fridge for up to 6 weeks.

PINE TIP SYRUP

Makes enough dashes for approximately 15 drinks

INGREDIENTS

200 ml (7 oz) water

100 g (3½ oz) unrefined demerara, cane or granulated (raw) sugar

handful of freshly picked pine tips (the little bright green leaves from spruce or pine trees, rather than the dark green, older leaves)

1 tablespoon corn syrup or golden syrup (optional)

EQUIPMENT Non-stick saucepan, wooden spoon, 200 ml (7 oz) kilner jar or glass bottle with stopper and a funnel

METHOD Boil the water in a non-stick saucepan and gently add the sugar and pine tips. Turn down the heat and stir constantly with a wooden spoon for 3–5 minutes, until all the sugar is dissolved and the syrup is clear. Turn off the heat and leave to cool. While still runny, pour into a sterilised kilner jar or funnel into a sterilised glass bottle with stopper. Adding a spoonful of corn syrup to the cooled mixture will help keep the syrup smooth. Store in the fridge for up to 6 weeks.

OTHER FLAVOURED SYRUPS

Using Simple Syrup (page 45) as the base, make your own infusions, tweaking amounts to taste according to the potency of your flavourings. A sprig or two for rosemary syrup should do it, whereas mint syrup needs a good handful. It's not an exact science.

Brown Sugar & Molasses
Basil & Lime
Cinnamon
Ginger & Cardamom
Honey
Ground Coffee
Mint
Pink Peppercorn
Rhubarb
Rosemary
Sage
Vanilla Bean

SOURS

Sours – a citrus-based mix that can include sugar syrup and egg white – cut through the gloopy sweetness of liqueurs. Shaken up with egg white and sugar syrup, a hit of fresh lemon and lime juice, or grapefruit and blood orange, is the fizzing topnote of recipes like the classic Sour. But a simple half-measure of lemon juice stirred through any sweet concoction will also do the trick, turning a grandma's snifter into something otherworldly.

SIMPLE SOUR MIX

INGREDIENTS

15 ml (½ oz) lemon juice, freshly squeezed

15 ml (½ oz) lime juice, freshly squeezed

METHOD
Mix both juices and deploy.

CLASSIC SOUR MIX

INGREDIENTS

15 ml (½ oz) lemon juice, freshly squeezed

15 ml (½ oz) lime juice, freshly squeezed

15 ml (½ oz) Simple Syrup (page 45)

1 egg white

EQUIPMENT Shaker

METHOD Mix both juices, the sugar syrup and egg white together and shake over ice with your chosen spirit.

BLOODY SOUR MIX

INGREDIENTS

15 ml (½ oz) blood orange juice, freshly squeezed

15 ml (½ oz) pink grapefruit juice, freshly squeezed

METHOD
Mix both juices and deploy.

BRINES

Brines: odd, salty infusions stolen from olive, caper and pickle jars add a savoury, acid kick to a drink, cutting through sweetness with more brute strength than citrus. But adding brine to an already hard, sharp liquor almost underlines its power. Olive brine mixed with a gin martini lends a deep, savoury kick; cocktail onions and a drop of vinegar add a sharp, acrid note, and a drop of pickle juice seems only to increase gin's firepower. The best bit? It's like having a drink and dinner in one, which, frankly, allows time for more drinking. There are no precise instructions or quantities here – add your choice of brine according to taste.

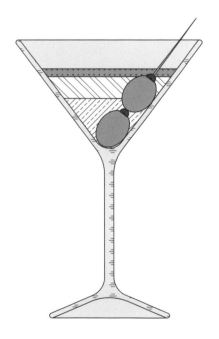

The Recipes

FROM ZINGY CLASSICS TO CONTEMPORARY
UPSTARTS SIZZLING WITH FLAVOUR – AND A FEW
CUCUMBER-SHAPED SURPRISES – GET READY TO
SHAKE, MUDDLE, AND STIR

GIN POWER SHOT

This little firecracker has a deceptive sweetness – fresh and zingy with a hot, spicy aftertaste. A reworking of a healthy breakfast pick-me-up, with a little gin thrown in – it really is the best way to start the day.

INGREDIENTS:

1	ginger juice, freshly squeezed	15 ml (½ oz)
2	gin	60 ml (2 oz)
3	cloudy apple juice	30 ml (1 oz)
4	lime juice, freshly squeezed	15 ml (½ oz)
5	homemade Simple Syrup (page 45)	dash
6	ginger slice	to garnish

EQUIPMENT Juicer (machine), shaker, strainer

METHOD Juice a thumb-sized piece of fresh ginger and add to a shaker with the remaining wet ingredients. Shake over ice. Add more Simple Syrup, to taste. Strain into a coupe and garnish with a slice of fresh ginger.

GLASS TYPE:
COUPE

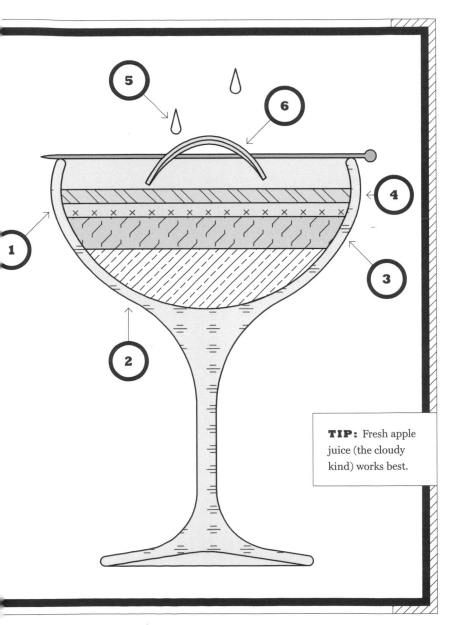

TIP: Fresh apple juice (the cloudy kind) works best.

SMASHED CUCUMBER

Cucumber and gin is a perfect combination, and the dill adds a sweet, if not slightly savoury, edge. Swap the dill for fennel tops or celery leaves if you want, but never mess with the cucumber.

INGREDIENTS

1	cucumber chunks	handful
2	cucumber juice, freshly juiced	30 ml (1 oz)
3	fresh dill	sprig
4	lime juice, freshly squeezed	15 ml (½ oz)
5	homemade Simple Syrup (page 45)	dash
6	gin	60 ml (2 oz)
7	chilled soda water	to top up
8	cucumber spear	to garnish

EQUIPMENT Muddler

METHOD In the glass, gently muddle a handful of cucumber chunks and the dill with the lime juice and simple syrup. Add the gin, cucumber juice and ice, top with chilled soda water and garnish with a cucumber spear.

GLASS TYPE:
HIGHBALL

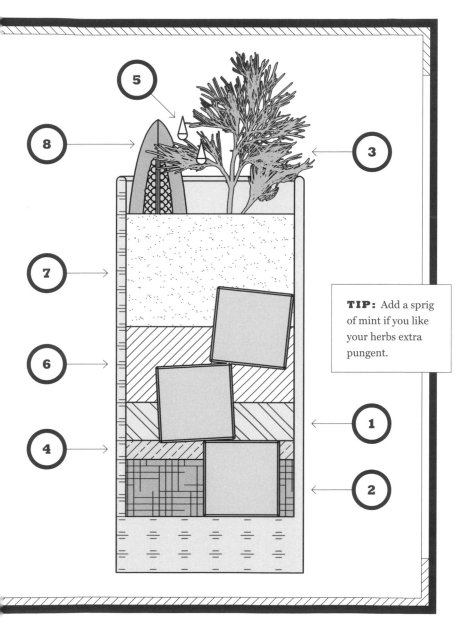

TIP: Add a sprig of mint if you like your herbs extra pungent.

PINE FOREST

Pine tips – the sweet, aromatic and bright green new needles at the end of fir twigs – make a delicious home-made syrup. Mix with gin and chilled nutty almond milk and you have yourself a delicious, sweet-smelling cocktail.

INGREDIENTS

1	gin	60 ml (2 oz)
2	almond milk	60 ml (2 oz)
3	homemade Pine Tip Syrup (page 48)	30 ml (½ oz)
4	pine tips	to garnish

EQUIPMENT Shaker

METHOD Shake the ingredients over ice, pour into a coupe and serve with freshly picked pine tips to garnish.

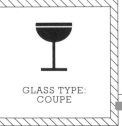

GLASS TYPE:
COUPE

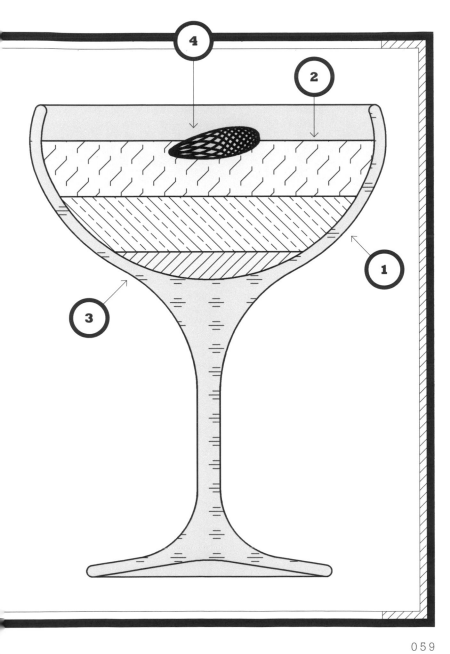

GRAPEFRUIT & TARRAGON COLLINS

The classic Gin Collins reworked with the soft anise flavour of fresh tarragon and the sharp tang of grapefruit. The grapefruit lends a soft pink tone and the tarragon adds a herby, liquorice aroma.

INGREDIENTS

1	fresh tarragon	3-4 blades
2	light brown sugar	1 tsp
3	gin	60 ml (2 oz)
4	pink or ruby grapefruit juice	60 ml (2 oz)
5	chilled tonic water	to top up
6	few blades of fresh tarragon	to garnish
7	grapefruit peel	to garnish

EQUIPMENT Muddler, shaker, strainer

METHOD Muddle the fresh tarragon and sugar in a shaker. Add a handful of ice cubes, the gin and grapefruit juice, shake and strain into a Collins glass full of ice. Top with chilled tonic water. Add a few blades of tarragon and grapefruit peel to garnish.

GLASS TYPE:
COLLINS

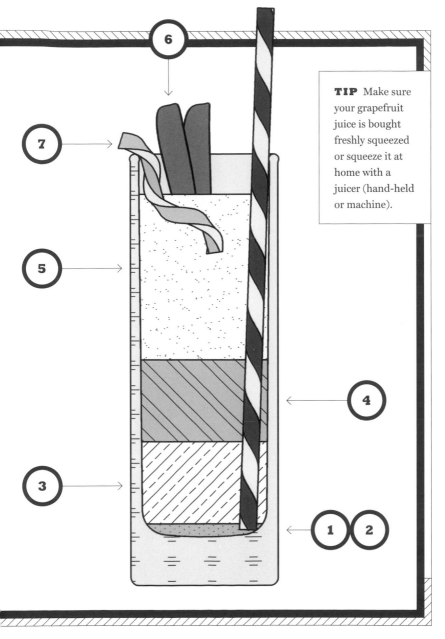

TIP Make sure your grapefruit juice is bought freshly squeezed or squeeze it at home with a juicer (hand-held or machine).

RHUBARB SOUR

A small, delicately pink and frothy cocktail that slaps you in the face with its tangy sour-sweetness. The acidic-stalked rhubarb plant is a mainstay of many an English garden, as are hedgehogs (they're not needed here – they taste awful).

INGREDIENTS

1	gin	60 ml (2 oz)
2	triple sec	30 ml (1 oz)
3	lemon juice, freshly squeezed	30 ml (1 oz)
4	homemade Rhubarb Syrup (page 49)	120 ml (4 oz)
5	egg white	1
6	orange peel	to garnish

EQUIPMENT Shaker, strainer

METHOD Shake the gin, triple sec, lemon juice, Rhubarb Syrup and egg white vigorously over ice. Strain into a coupe and garnish with orange peel.

GLASS TYPE:
COUPE

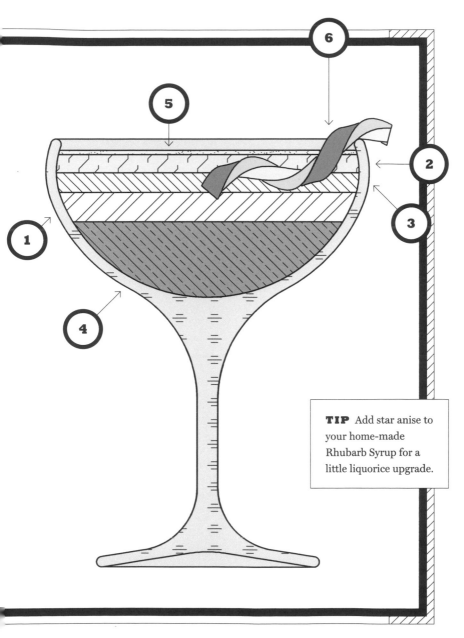

TIP Add star anise to your home-made Rhubarb Syrup for a little liquorice upgrade.

CUCUMBER LEMONADE

Imagine making a fresh, zingy and wholesome lemonade of the type seen at kids' lemonade stands across the world, with a sneaky shot of Mum and Dad's gin thrown in – and all the adults get smashed. And then something happens with a cucumber. That's this drink.

INGREDIENTS

1	gin	60 ml (2 oz)
2	cucumber juice, freshly squeezed	30 ml (1 oz)
3	lemon juice, freshly squeezed	15 ml (½ oz)
4	homemade Simple Syrup (page 45) or agave syrup	dash
5	cucumber spear	to garnish
6	chilled soda water	to top up

EQUIPMENT Shaker, strainer

METHOD Shake the gin, cucumber and lemon juices and syrup over ice. Add a cucumber spear and ice cubes to a highball glass, strain the drink and pour into the glass. Top with soda water.

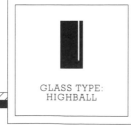

GLASS TYPE:
HIGHBALL

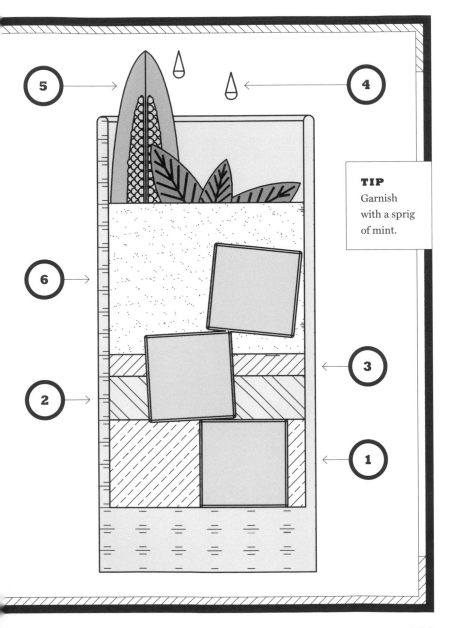

TIP
Garnish with a sprig of mint.

CHERRY THYME SOUR

A dark, rich cherry sour with a soft thyme aroma edged with sharp, freshly squeezed lime juice. Add the Angostura bitters at the end to cut through the pink-tinged foam.

INGREDIENTS

1	gin	60 ml (2 oz)
2	triple sec	30 ml (1 oz)
3	lime juice, freshly squeezed	30 ml (1 oz)
4	Cherry & Thyme Syrup (page 48)	120 ml (4 oz)
5	egg white	1
6	Angostura bitters	dash
7	fresh thyme sprig	to garnish

EQUIPMENT Shaker, strainer

METHOD Shake the gin, triple sec, lime juice, syrup and egg white vigorously over ice. Strain into a coupe, add a couple of drops of Angostura bitters and garnish with a sprig of thyme.

GLASS TYPE:
COUPE

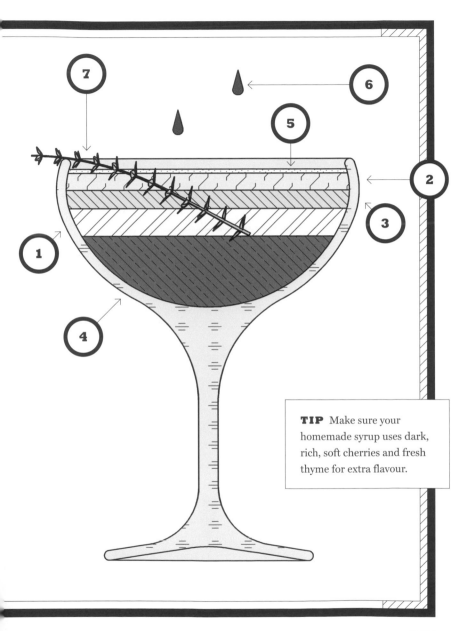

TIP Make sure your homemade syrup uses dark, rich, soft cherries and fresh thyme for extra flavour.

PINK GIN SPRITZ

For those who hanker for a **Negroni at breakfast** – but are embarrassed it looks a bit serious for 7:45 am. This delightfully rose-hued cocktail is topped with chilled pink grapefruit juice to mask your sins.

INGREDIENTS

1	gin	60 ml (2 oz)
2	Aperol	30 ml (1 oz)
3	Campari	15 ml (½ oz)
4	homemade Spiced Brown Sugar Syrup (page 47)	dash
5	chilled pink grapefruit juice	to top up

EQUIPMENT Shaker

METHOD Shake the gin, Aperol, Campari and Brown Sugar Syrup over ice. Add to a Champagne flute and top with the chilled pink grapefruit juice.

GLASS TYPE:
CHAMPAGNE
FLUTE

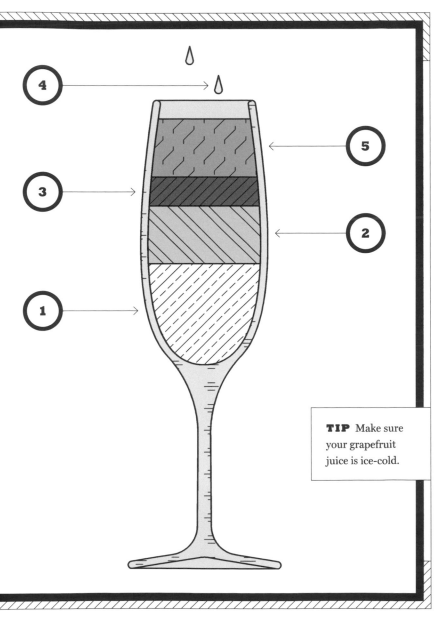

TIP Make sure
your grapefruit
juice is ice-cold.

NAKED PEACH

Pink, soft, and hairy – the humble peach forms the base of this
concoction, and roasting it brings out its sweetness. Rosemary is
an odd addition, but it really works. The sharp lime binds it all together
and the generous sugar content makes it rather moreish.

INGREDIENTS

1	large roasted or very ripe peach (see tip)	1
2	light brown sugar	1 tsp
3	lime juice, freshly squeezed	15 ml (½ oz)
4	gin	60 ml (2 oz)
5	lime zest	pinch
6	homemade Rosemary Syrup (page 49)	15 ml (½ oz)
7	chilled lemonade	to top up
8	peach slices	to garnish
9	rosemary	to garnish

EQUIPMENT Blender, sieve, shaker

METHOD Purée the roasted peach, sugar and lime juice in a blender, then
sieve. Shake the gin, peach purée, lime zest
and syrup over ice and add to a coupe. Top
with chilled lemonade and garnish with peach
slices and rosemary.

GLASS TYPE:
COUPE

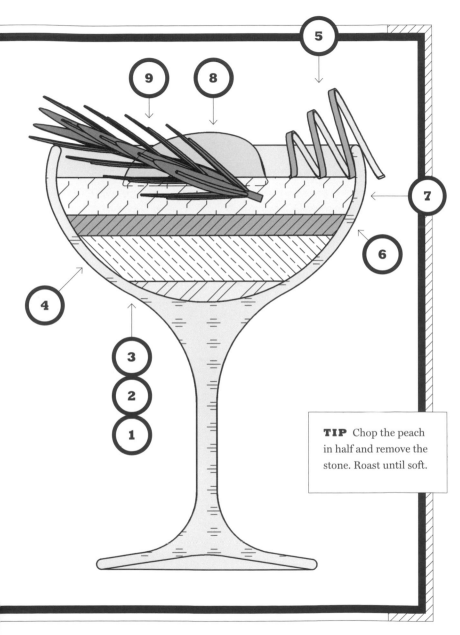

TIP Chop the peach in half and remove the stone. Roast until soft.

LONG ISLAND ICED TEA

A cup of hot tea and a little drop of gin and vodka just seems, well, dirty. Throw out the tea and add an embarrassing amount of alcohol and ice and you apparently have yourself a rather classy, artful drink.

INGREDIENTS:

1	gin	30 ml (1 oz)
2	vodka	30 ml (1 oz)
3	light rum	30 ml (1 oz)
4	tequila	30 ml (1 oz)
5	lemon juice, freshly squeezed	30 ml (1 oz)
6	orange liqueur	30 ml (1 oz)
7	cola	splash
8	lime slices	to garnish
9	lemon slices	to garnish

EQUIPMENT Bar spoon

METHOD: Pour the ingredients into a glass filled with ice cubes. Stir with the spoon and add the citrus slices. Serve with a straw.

GLASS TYPE:
HIGHBALL

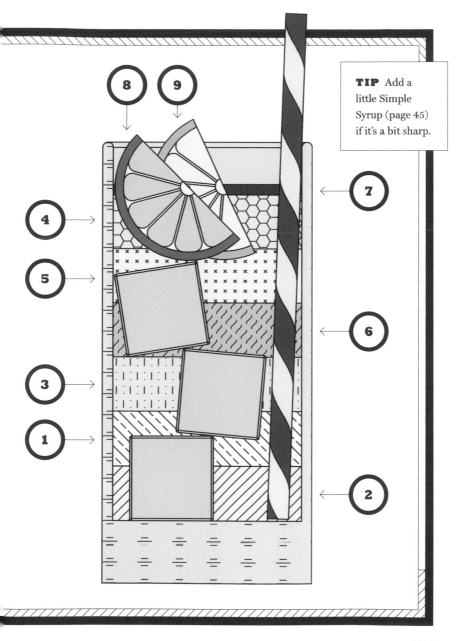

TIP Add a little Simple Syrup (page 45) if it's a bit sharp.

073

GIN RICKEY

Simple, sharp, refreshing and – after a couple – dizzying. Tweak the balance between sugar and lime to taste, but a good Rickey should be bright, zingy and strong.

INGREDIENTS

1	gin	60 ml (2 oz)
2	lime juice, freshly squeezed	1 tbsp
3	homemade Simple Syrup (page 45)	1 tbsp
4	soda water	to top up
5	lime wedge	to garnish

EQUIPMENT Bar spoon

METHOD Pour the gin, lime juice and syrup into a highball glass filled with ice cubes. Stir then top up with soda water and garnish with a lime wedge. Serve with a straw.

GLASS TYPE:
HIGHBALL

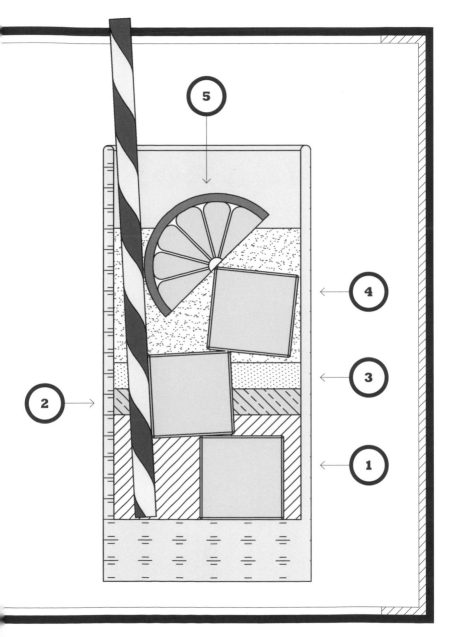

NEGRONI

The tougher, more intense version of the Americano, created in Florence, where a hero of the cocktail world thought to replace soda water with gin. What a marvellous man!

INGREDIENTS

1	gin	30 ml (1 oz)
2	sweet vermouth	30 ml (1 oz)
3	Campari	60 ml (2 oz)
4	twist of orange peel	to garnish

EQUIPMENT Mixing glass, strainer

METHOD Stir the gin, vermouth and Campari in a mixing glass over ice. Strain into a tumbler over a block of ice. Garnish with the orange peel.

GLASS TYPE:
TUMBLER

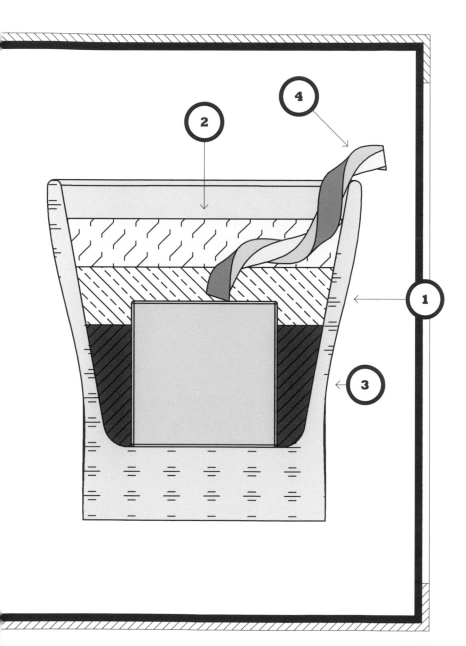

077

GIMLET

The original gin and juice – a power-punch of a cocktail. You can swap the lime juice for any other acidic fruit.

INGREDIENTS

1	gin	60 ml (2 oz)
2	lime juice, freshly squeezed	15 ml (½ oz)

EQUIPMENT Shaker, strainer

METHOD Shake the ingredients with ice and vigour and strain into a chilled martini glass or coupe with a couple of ice cubes.

GLASS TYPE:
COUPE
OR MARTINI

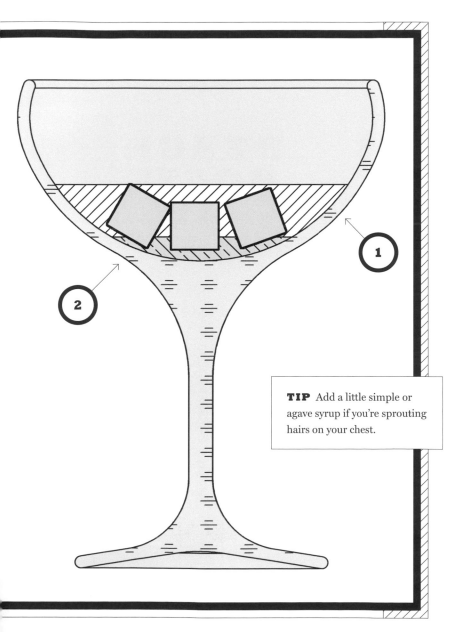

TIP Add a little simple or agave syrup if you're sprouting hairs on your chest.

BEACH HOUSE

This Barbadian classic is covertly tropical. It has the appearance of a simple G & T, but with coconut water instead of tonic. Fresh and sweet, this little number tastes deceptively alcohol-light.

INGREDIENTS

1	gin	60 ml (2 oz)
2	lime juice, freshly squeezed	15 ml (½ oz)
3	chilled coconut water	to top up
4	lime slice	to garnish

EQUIPMENT Swizzle stick

METHOD Pour the gin and lime juice into a highball glass over crushed ice, top with coconut water and add a swizzle stick and lime slice to garnish.

GLASS TYPE:
HIGHBALL

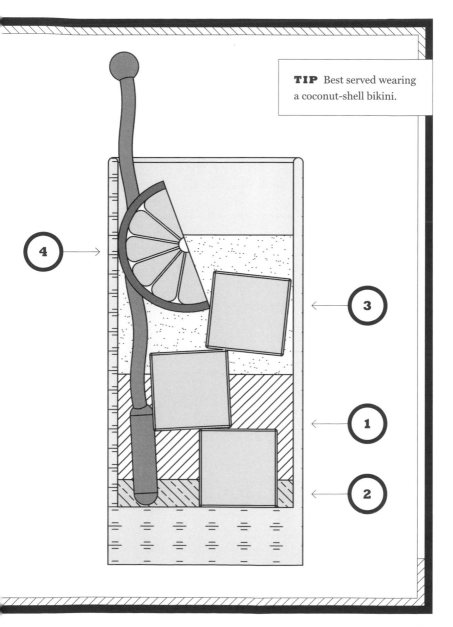

TIP Best served wearing a coconut-shell bikini.

BERGAMOT TEA MARTINI

Temperature is essential for this one – the iciness will mellow out the spirits and lift the bergamot oil-infused tea leaves to new heights. Keep it classy, otherwise it's just a couple of shots of booze with a teabag thrown in. It's all in the eye of the beholder.

INGREDIENTS

1	gin	30 ml (1 oz)
2	vodka	30 ml (1 oz)
3	premium Earl Grey teabag	1
4	orange bitters	dash
5	orange peel	to garnish

EQUIPMENT Shaker

METHOD Pour the gin and vodka over a premium Earl Grey teabag at room temperature. Allow to steep for at least 30 minutes, then remove the teabag. Add the bitters, shake vigorously over ice and serve in a tiki or glass mug with orange peel to garnish.

GLASS TYPE:
TIKI OR GLASS
MUG

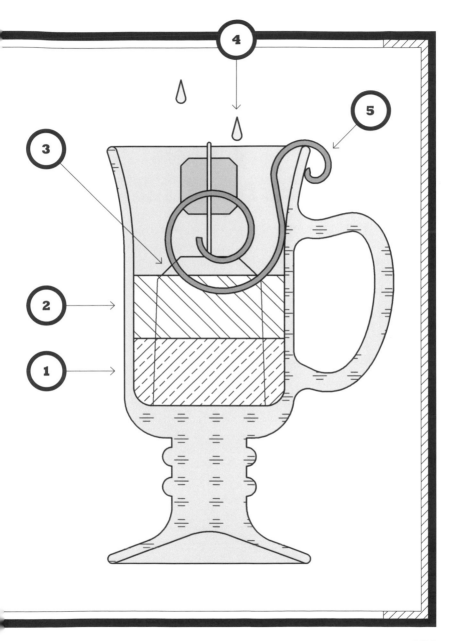

CUCUMBER MINT GIN FIZZ

You can do almost anything with a cucumber, but this is definitely in the top five. The secret is to infuse the gin for as long as possible and to serve the whole thing super-chilled.

INGREDIENTS

1	fresh mint sprig	1
2	cucumber, cut into spears	1
3	gin	60 ml (2 oz)
4	lemon juice, freshly squeezed	dash
5	chilled tonic water	to top up

EQUIPMENT Muddler, jug, strainer

METHOD Bruise the mint sprig using a muddler, and add to the jug with most of the cucumber spears. Cover with the gin and chill for 2 hours in the fridge. Fill a highball or tumbler with a few ice cubes, add a fresh cucumber spear and the lemon juice and strain the chilled, infused gin into the glass. Top with chilled tonic water.

GLASS TYPE:
HIGHBALL
OR TUMBLER

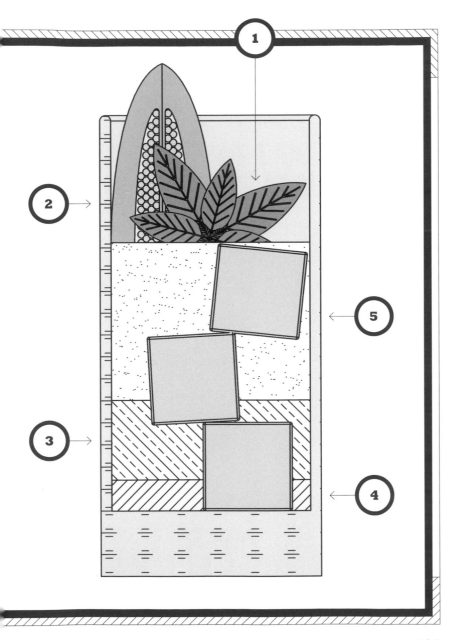

GINGER GREYHOUND

Refreshingly simple, a classic Greyhound only has two elements – gin and juice – but this version includes a little spicy ginger syrup to add warmth and take the edge off.

INGREDIENTS

1	gin	60 ml (2 oz)
2	grapefruit juice, freshly squeezed	100 ml (3½ oz)
3	homemade Spiced Brown Sugar Syrup (page 47)	dash
4	crystallised ginger, grated	to garnish

EQUIPMENT Shaker

METHOD Shake the wet ingredients with ice cubes and vigour and pour into a chilled coupe or martini glass. Top with the grated crystallised ginger.

GLASS TYPE:
COUPE
OR MARTINI

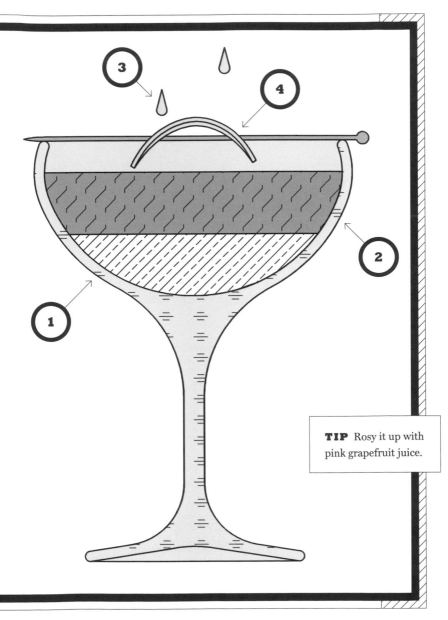

TIP Rosy it up with pink grapefruit juice.

HONEY BEER PUNCH

A sweet, beery take on Long Island Iced Tea with gin, honey and a premium brew creating a slip-down punch for one. Add more honey to taste.

INGREDIENTS

1	honey	1 tsp
2	hot water	splash
3	lemon juice, freshly squeezed	15 ml (½ oz)
4	gin	60 ml (2 oz)
5	chilled premium beer	to top up
6	lemon slice	to garnish

EQUIPMENT Mixing glass

METHOD Melt a generous teaspoon of honey in a mixing glass with a splash of hot water and allow to cool. Add to a tall glass filled with ice, lemon juice and gin. Stir and top with chilled beer, adding a lemon slice to garnish.

GLASS TYPE:
HIGHBALL

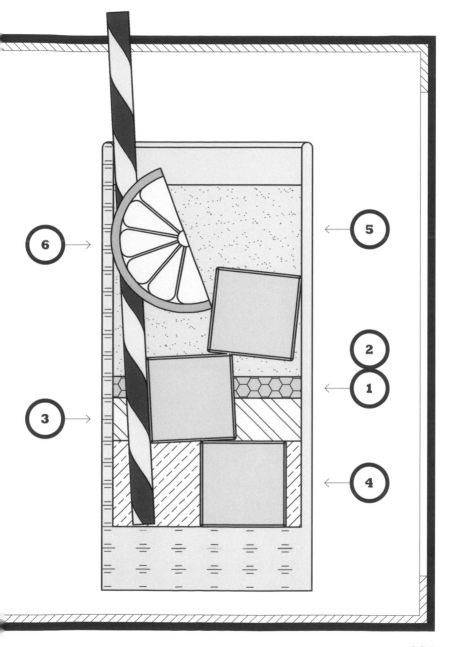

GILBERT GRAPE

Roasting the grapes gives them a deep, golden sultana flavour – a little like a dessert wine – and fresh thyme lends a herby aroma. Ginger adds a spicy little kick.

INGREDIENTS

1	green seedless grapes	handful
2	fresh thyme sprigs	2-3
3	light brown sugar	1 tbsp
4	gin	60 ml (2 oz)
5	homemade Spiced Brown Sugar Syrup (page 47)	30 ml (1 oz)
6	lime juice, freshly squeezed	15 ml (½ oz)
7	chilled soda water	to top up
8	fresh thyme sprig	to garnish

EQUIPMENT Muddler, shaker, strainer

METHOD Roast the grapes whole until soft and caramelised. Allow to cool, then muddle them with the thyme and sugar. Add the gin, sugar syrup and lime juice and shake. Strain into a highball full of ice and top with soda water. Garnish with more fresh thyme sprigs.

GLASS TYPE:
HIGHBALL

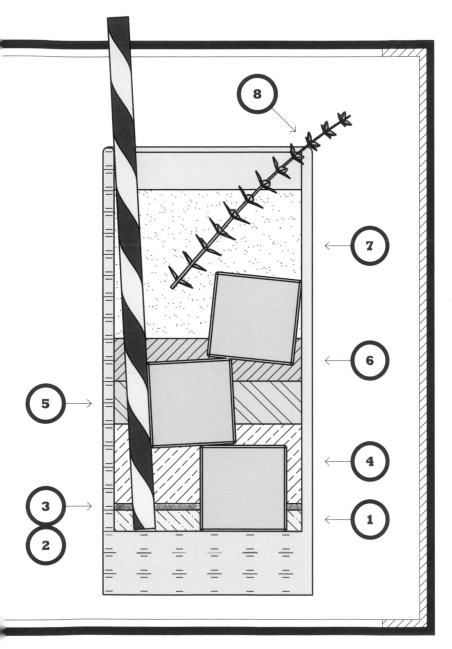

SPICED RHUBARB & ROSE RAMOS GIN FIZZ

Inspired by legendary cocktail maker Henry C. Ramos, who created the Ramos Gin Fizz in New Orleans, 1888, this is perhaps the campest cocktail in the book. This pastel-pink drink – with its delicately perfumed aroma – is unashamedly delicious. It's like a scantily-clad slumber party in a glass.

INGREDIENTS

1	gin	60 ml (2 oz)
2	homemade Rhubarb, Ginger & Star Anise Syrup (page 46)	60 ml (2 oz)
3	single (light) cream	30 ml (1 oz)
4	lime juice, freshly squeezed	15 ml (½ oz)
5	lemon juice, freshly squeezed	15 ml (½ oz)
6	egg white	1
7	rosewater	dash
8	chilled soda water	to top up

EQUIPMENT Shaker, strainer

METHOD Shake the wet ingredients – except the soda water – for 30 seconds, then add ice and shake for another 30 seconds. Strain into a coupe and top with soda water.

GLASS TYPE:
COUPE

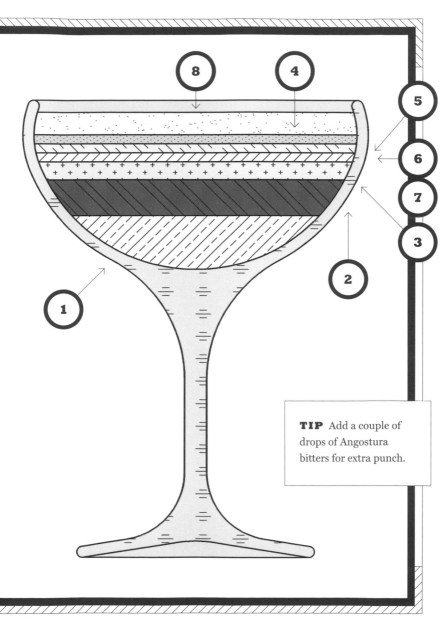

TIP Add a couple of drops of Angostura bitters for extra punch.

ELDERFLOWER MARTINI

The classic gin martini reworked with St-Germain, the elderflower liqueur. Lemon juice cuts through the sweetness and mint leaves give a fresh, herby aroma.

INGREDIENTS

1	gin	30 ml (1 oz)
2	vodka	30 ml (1 oz)
3	St-Germain	30 ml (1 oz)
4	lemon juice, freshly squeezed	15 ml (½ oz)
5	fresh mint sprig	to garnish

EQUIPMENT Shaker, strainer

METHOD Shake the wet ingredients over ice and strain into a martini glass or coupe. Garnish with a mint sprig.

GLASS TYPE:
MARTINI
OR COUPE

TIP Add a dash of mint syrup or Simple Syrup (page 45), to taste.

SLOE GIN & TEMPRANILLO NEGRONI

Rich, sloe-berry-infused gin with a sweet, dark Tempranillo reduction make this a potent, wintry spin on the ultimate summer cocktail.

INGREDIENTS

1	Sloe & Star Anise Gin (page 42)	30 ml (1 oz)
2	Tempranillo Reduction (page 44)	30 ml (1 oz)
3	Campari	60 ml (2 oz)
4	orange peel	to garnish

EQUIPMENT Mixing glass, strainer

METHOD Stir the ingredients in a mixing glass over ice. Strain into a tumbler filled with ice cubes. Garnish with the orange peel.

GLASS TYPE:
TUMBLER

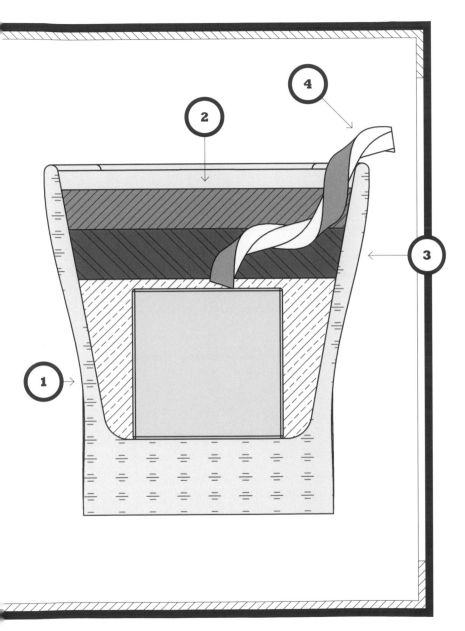

GOOSEBERRY GIN FIZZ

Gooseberries are evil little fruits: lurid green, veiny-looking and sour as acid, but muddled with brown sugar they turn into something wonderful. This classic gin fizz is sweet, subtly perfumed and sizzlingly tart.

INGREDIENTS

1	fresh gooseberries	handful
2	light brown sugar	1 tbsp
3	gin	60 ml (2 oz)
4	elderflower cordial	30 ml (1 oz)
5	lime juice, freshly squeezed	15 ml (½ oz)
6	chilled cloudy sparkling lemonade	to top up
7	fresh gooseberries	to garnish

EQUIPMENT Muddler, shaker, strainer

METHOD Muddle the gooseberries and sugar together, add the gin, elderflower cordial and lime juice and shake. Strain into a highball full of ice and top with lemonade. Garnish with fresh, sliced gooseberries.

GLASS TYPE:
HIGHBALL

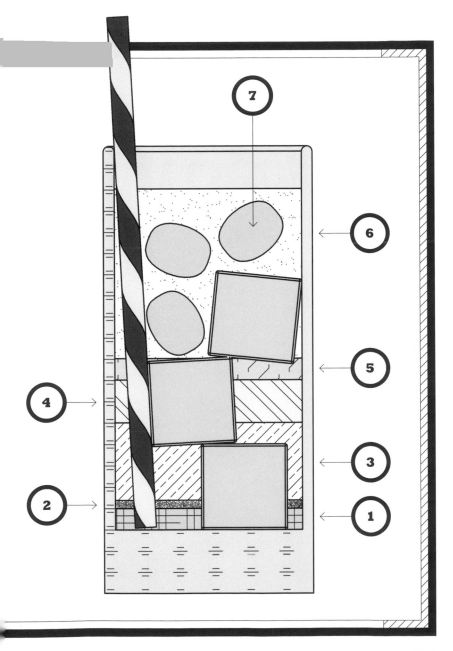

099

BAY LEAF & GREEN TEA MARTINI

The classic martini, underpinned with an excellent, high-quality and super-dry gin, with a bay and green tea flavour adding a fresh, verdant and rather firm woodiness.

INGREDIENTS

1	premium green tea teabag	1
2	vodka	30 ml (1 oz)
3	Bay Leaf Gin (page 43)	60 ml (2 oz)
4	lemon juice, freshly squeezed	15 ml (½ oz)
5	fresh bay leaf	to garnish

EQUIPMENT Shaker, strainer

METHOD Steep the green tea teabag in the vodka and at room temperature for 30 minutes. Remove the teabag. Shake the wet ingredients over ice and strain into a glass. Top with the lemon juice and garnish with a bay leaf.

GLASS TYPE:
MARTINI OR COUPE OR
TUMBLER

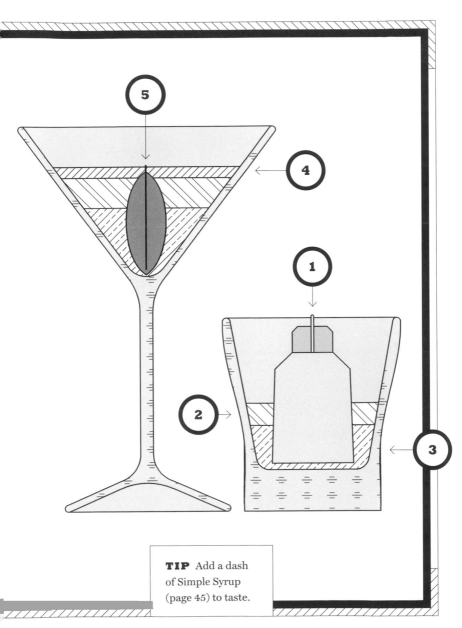

TIP Add a dash of Simple Syrup (page 45) to taste.

THE QUEEN MUM

Gin and Dubonnet (the sweet, wine-based aperitif) is thought to have been the Queen Mother's favourite tipple, and who are we to disagree? Think of this potent royal cocktail as a sweet Negroni with a fragrant orange blossom bouquet.

INGREDIENTS

1	gin	60 ml (2 oz)
2	Dubonnet	60 ml (2 oz)
3	orange blossom water	dash
4	Angostura bitters	dash
5	orange peel	to garnish

EQUIPMENT Mixing glass, strainer

METHOD Add the wet ingredients to a mixing glass and stir with ice, then strain into a tumbler or coupe with a rock of ice. Garnish with a large piece of orange peel.

GLASS TYPE:
TUMBLER
OR COUPE

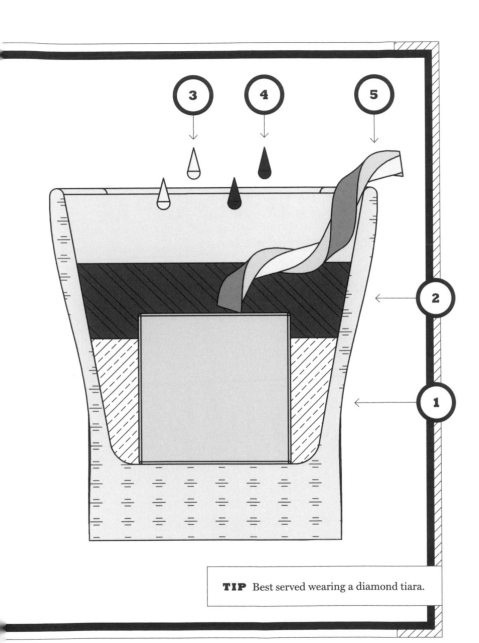

TIP Best served wearing a diamond tiara.

THE RUDOLPH

Gin, elderflower liqueur and chilled Champagne: a perfect festive season cocktail with a string of Rudolph noses for added schmaltz. Looks great in a martini glass, or coupe.

INGREDIENTS

1	gin	60 ml (2 oz)
2	St-Germain	30 ml (1 oz)
3	chilled Champagne	to top up
4	string of fresh redcurrants	to garnish

METHOD Pour the gin and St-Germain into a chilled martini glass or coupe, top with Champagne and garnish with a string of fresh redcurrants.

GLASS TYPE:
COUPE
OR MARTINI

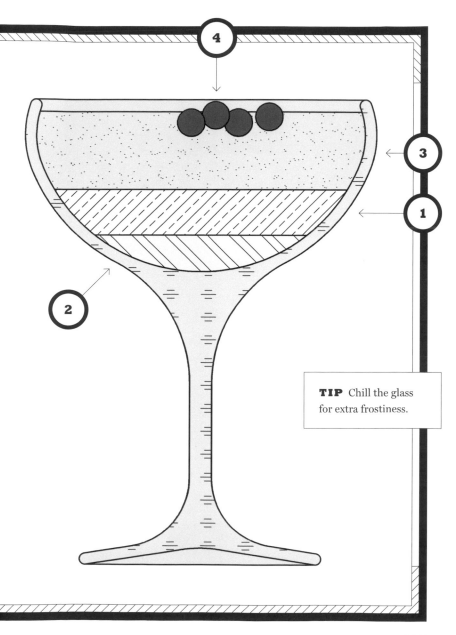

TIP Chill the glass for extra frostiness.

DIRTY MARTINI

This is one of the very best ways to drink gin: perfectly chilled, aromatic and underpinned with a little dry vermouth and the tang of brine. Use a good, gourmet olive or caperberry and be generous with the brine. You'll wince as it goes down. Absolutely filthy.

INGREDIENTS

1	gin	60 ml (2 oz)
2	dry vermouth	30 ml (1 oz)
3	olive brine	to taste
4	olives	to garnish

EQUIPMENT Shaker, strainer

METHOD Shake the gin and vermouth over ice, strain and pour into a martini glass or coupe. Spoon in the brine and add an olive or two.

GLASS TYPE:
MARTINI
OR COUPE

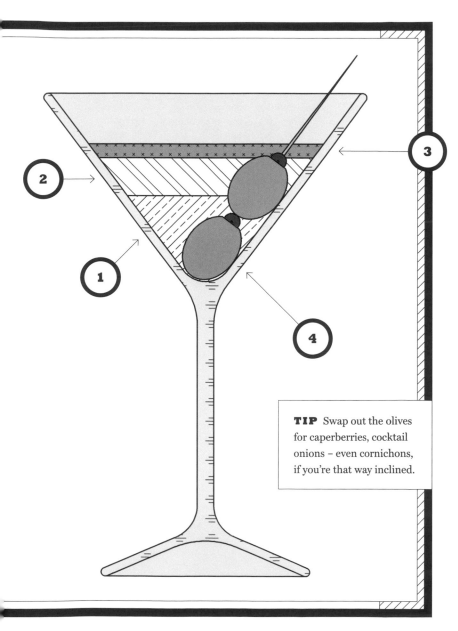

1

2

3

4

TIP Swap out the olives for caperberries, cocktail onions – even cornichons, if you're that way inclined.

SUMMER BLUEBERRY COCKTAIL

The blender cocktail: a no-fuss, all-in-one cocktail with a bright purple hue, flecked with aromatic fresh herbs. Use frozen blueberries and it's summer all year around.

INGREDIENTS

1	gin	60 ml (2 oz)
2	vodka	30 ml (1 oz)
3	frozen blueberries	large handful
4	lime juice, freshly squeezed	15 ml (½ oz)
5	homemade Mint Syrup (page 49)	dash
6	fresh mint leaves	8–10 leaves
7	chilled mineral water	to loosen
8	fresh mint sprig	to garnish
9	few whole blueberries	to garnish

EQUIPMENT Blender, wide straw

METHOD Whizz the gin, vodka, blueberries, lime juice, syrup and mint leaves in a blender, then add a little chilled mineral water to loosen the liquid. Pour into a highball full of ice, garnish with a mint sprig, a few whole blueberries and serve with a straw.

GLASS TYPE:
HIGHBALL

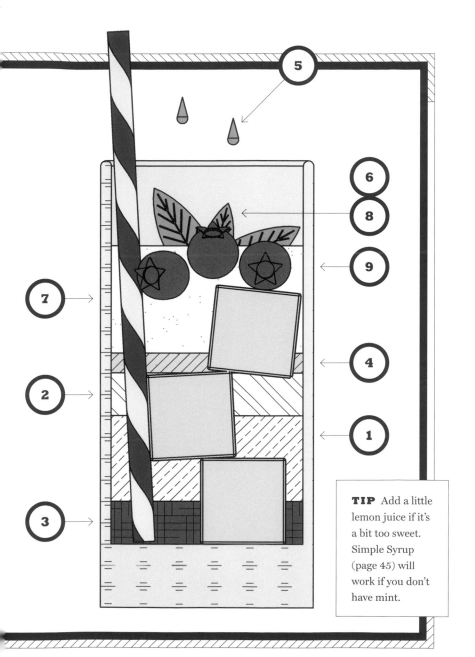

TIP Add a little lemon juice if it's a bit too sweet. Simple Syrup (page 45) will work if you don't have mint.

THE COLBY

This dry, ruby-hued cocktail with a little elderflower is a reworked Cosmo and is extremely potent. Named after the world's finest red-headed actor, Colby Keller. A cocktail with real muscle.

INGREDIENTS

1	gin	60 ml (2 oz)
2	St-Germain	30 ml (1 oz)
3	lemon juice, freshly squeezed	15 ml (½ oz)
4	cranberry juice	90 ml (3 oz)
5	orange bitters	dash
6	fresh cranberries	to garnish

EQUIPMENT Shaker, strainer

METHOD Shake the wet ingredients over ice, strain into a martini glass, tumbler or coupe and garnish with fresh cranberries.

GLASS TYPE:
MARTINI, TUMBLER
OR COUPE

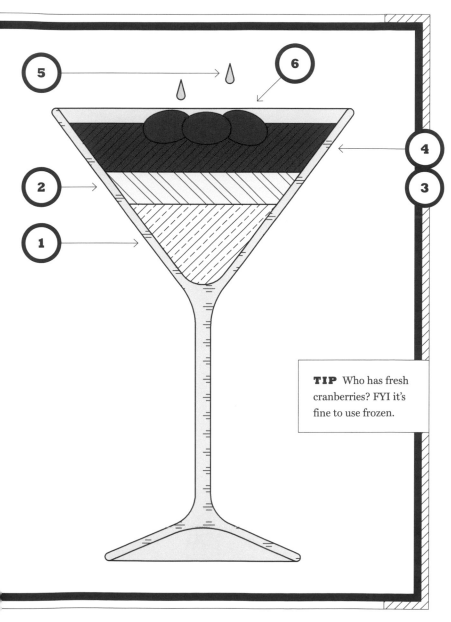

TIP Who has fresh cranberries? FYI it's fine to use frozen.

BRAMBLE

Imagine an autumnal English hedgerow liquidised into a glass. This fresh berry-studded and herby cocktail is best served over crushed ice – or make it long with chilled soda water.

INGREDIENTS

1	fresh blackberries	handful
2	gin	60 ml (2 oz)
3	lemon juice, freshly squeezed	15 ml (½ oz)
4	homemade Simple Syrup (page 45)	splash
5	crushed ice	handful
6	crème de mûre	splash
7	fresh blackberries	to garnish
8	fresh mint sprig	to garnish

EQUIPMENT Muddler

METHOD Gently muddle the handful of fresh blackberries with gin, lemon juice and syrup in a glass. Add crushed ice and a generous splash of crème de mûre. Garnish with fresh blackberries and mint.

GLASS TYPE:
TUMBLER
OR HIGHBALL

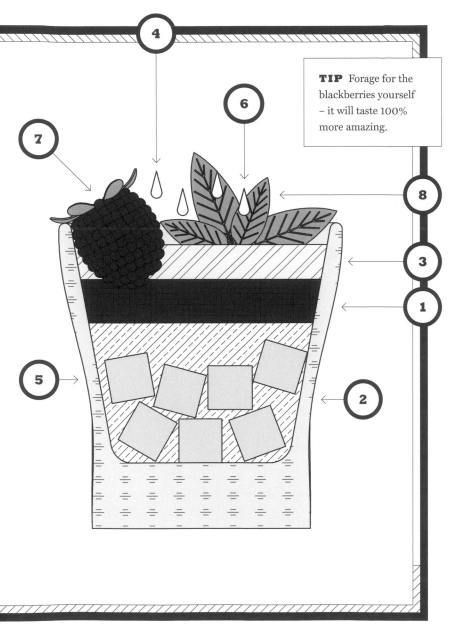

TIP Forage for the blackberries yourself – it will taste 100% more amazing.

CHERRY FRENCH 75

This drink combines two wonderful things: being French and an obsession with cherry popping. This classic cocktail, with a fruity upgrade, is fresh and sharp with a little fizz for good measure.

INGREDIENTS

1	ripe, stoned small cherries	handful
2	Cherry Heering liqueur	15 ml (½ oz)
3	lemon juice, freshly squeezed	15 ml (½ oz)
4	rosewater	dash
5	gin	60 ml (2 oz)
6	chilled Prosecco	to top up
7	cherry	to garnish

EQUIPMENT Muddler, shaker, strainer

METHOD Gently muddle the cherries, Cherry Heering, lemon juice and rosewater. Add the gin and shake over ice.
Strain into a coupe or martini glass and top with chilled Prosecco.
Garnish with a single cherry.

GLASS TYPE:
COUPE
OR MARTINI

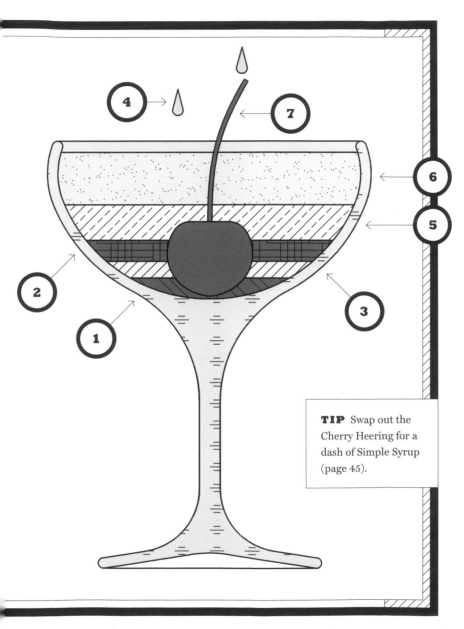

TIP Swap out the Cherry Heering for a dash of Simple Syrup (page 45).

THE GIBSON

This drink will put hairs on your chest. And onion on your breath. Think of it as a classic Martini soured with cocktail onions – try it with a little pickle juice if you're tough enough. Because of the simplicity of the recipe, pick a premium gin.

INGREDIENTS

1	gin	60 ml (2 oz)
2	dry vermouth	15 ml (½ oz)
3	cocktail onions	2–3, to garnish

EQUIPMENT Shaker

METHOD Shake the gin and dry vermouth over ice, pour into a chilled glass and add 2–3 cocktail onions.

GLASS TYPE:
MARTINI
OR COUPE

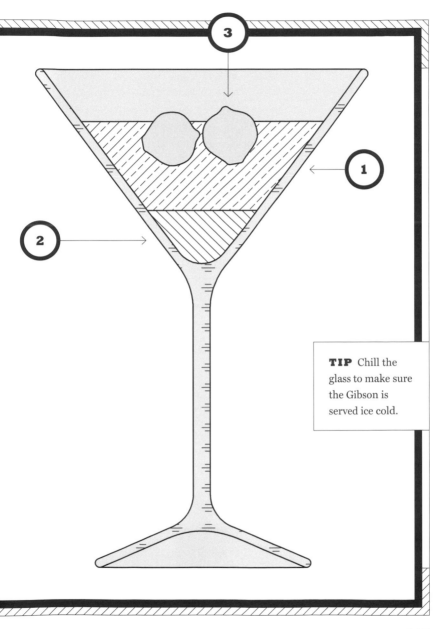

TIP Chill the glass to make sure the Gibson is served ice cold.

NEW FASHIONED

This version of the classic Old Fashioned swaps out whiskey for a premium gin; the bitters give the drink a pale gold colour. Make sure your gin is extra fragrant, your lime peel is fresh and pungent and your ice is lumpy and jagged.

INGREDIENTS

1	really excellent gin	60 ml (2 oz)
2	homemade Simple Syrup (page 45)	splash
3	Angostura bitters	dash
4	orange bitters	dash
5	large strip of lime peel	to garnish

METHOD Add the gin and syrup to a heavy-bottomed tumbler over a large piece of ice. Splash the bitters on top and garnish with a large strip of lime peel.

GLASS TYPE:
TUMBLER

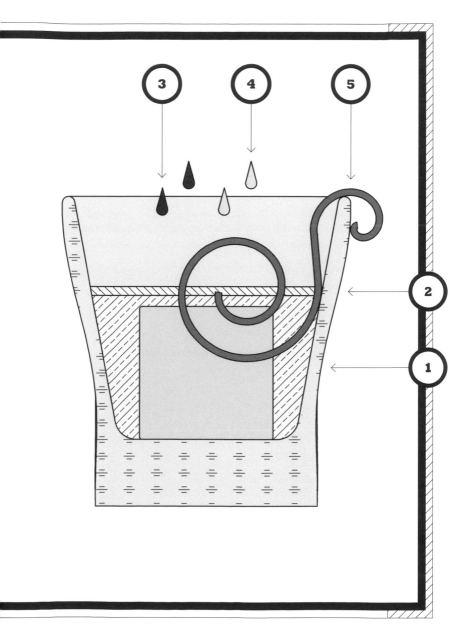

PERFECT GIN & TONIC

The most perfect drink in the world. Each gin-lover has their own way of making this classic cocktail – but the secret is to keep it simple. Oh, and don't forget to dial up the citrus aroma with fresh lime juice and a drop or two of orange bitters.

INGREDIENTS

1	gin	60 ml (2 oz)
2	lime juice, freshly squeezed	splash
3	cucumber spear	to garnish
4	chilled premium tonic water	to top up
5	orange bitters	dash

EQUIPMENT Bar spoon

METHOD Add the gin, lime juice and cucumber spear to a highball filled with ice cubes and stir with a spoon. Top with chilled premium tonic and add a dash of orange bitters. Serve with a straw.

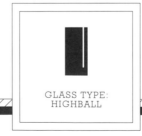

GLASS TYPE:
HIGHBALL

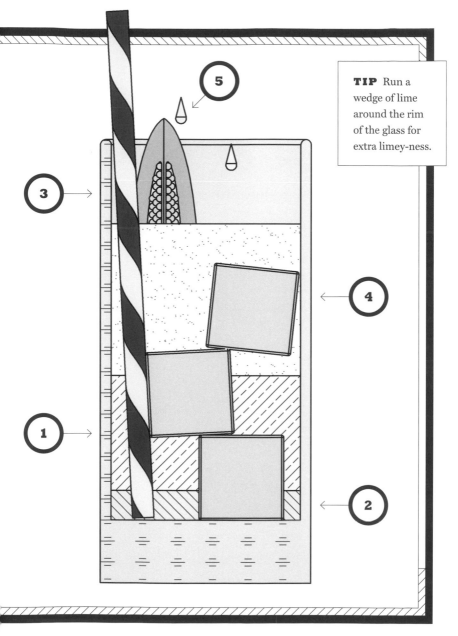

TIP Run a wedge of lime around the rim of the glass for extra limey-ness.

WATERMELON GIN & TONIC

A classic cocktail transformed with fresh watermelon, elderflower tonic, mint and a dry premium gin. Serve this at summer back yard barbecues and watch as the adults take over the kids' trampoline. Powerful stuff.

INGREDIENTS

1	gin	60 ml (2 oz)
2	watermelon juice, freshly squeezed	60 ml (2 oz)
3	lemon juice, freshly squeezed	dash
4	chilled premium elderflower tonic water	to top up
5	small wedge of watermelon	to garnish
6	fresh mint sprig	to garnish

EQUIPMENT Shaker, strainer

METHOD Shake the gin, freshly squeezed watermelon juice and lemon juice over ice. Strain into a highball filled with ice and top with tonic water. Garnish with a small wedge of watermelon and mint. Serve with a straw.

GLASS TYPE:
HIGHBALL

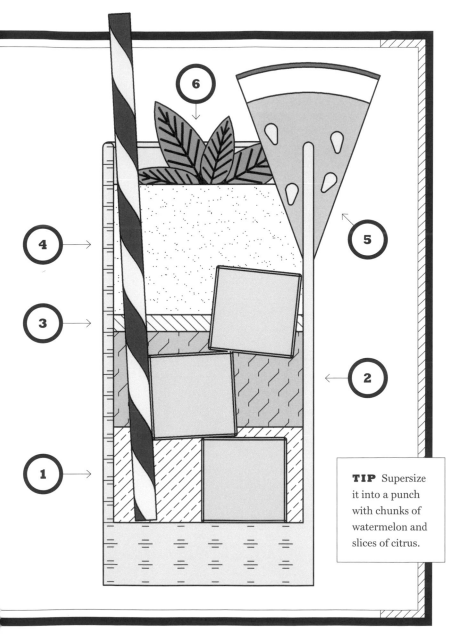

TIP Supersize it into a punch with chunks of watermelon and slices of citrus.

BLOOD ORANGE GIN & TONIC

A ruby-red, citrussy gin & tonic with a little ginger syrup for a spicy uplift. Use premium tonic water – or ginger beer, if you like it spicy.

INGREDIENTS

1	gin	60 ml (2 oz)
2	homemade Spiced Brown Sugar Syrup (page 47)	dash
3	blood orange juice, freshly squeezed	60 ml (2 oz)
4	lime juice, freshly squeezed	dash
5	chilled premium tonic water	to top up
6	orange peel	to garnish

EQUIPMENT Shaker, strainer

METHOD Shake the gin, syrup, blood orange juice and lime juice over ice. Strain into a highball glass filled with ice and top with chilled premium tonic water. Garnish with orange peel.

GLASS TYPE:
HIGHBALL

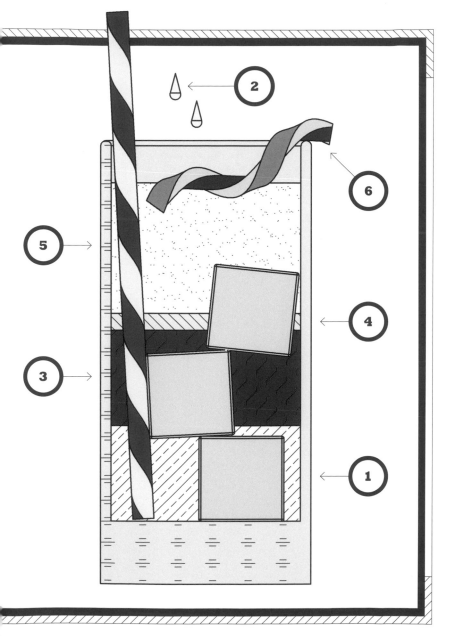

THE SOUTHSIDE

This Prohibition classic is said to have originated at the 21 Club in NYC, inspired by a long version served over crushed ice drunk by Chicago mobsters. It's fresh, zingy and slightly illegal-tasting.

INGREDIENTS

1	fresh mint sprigs	2–3
2	gin	60 ml (2 oz)
3	lime, freshly squeezed	30 ml (1 oz)
4	homemade Simple Syrup (page 45)	15 ml (½ oz)
5	fresh mint sprig	to garnish

EQUIPMENT Muddler, shaker, strainer

METHOD Softly bruise the mint using a muddler. Shake the ingredients over ice and strain into a martini glass or coupe. Garnish with a fresh mint sprig.

GLASS TYPE:
COUPE
OR MARTINI

TIP Dress like a 1930s mobster before you take your first sip.

WHITE LADY

The zingy classic cocktail with notes of orange and a power punch of lemon juice. Simple, powerful and rather sharp.

INGREDIENTS

1	gin	60 ml (2 oz)
2	Cointreau	15 ml (½ oz)
3	lemon juice, freshly squeezed	15 ml (½ oz)

EQUIPMENT Shaker

METHOD Shake over ice and serve.

GLASS TYPE:
COUPE

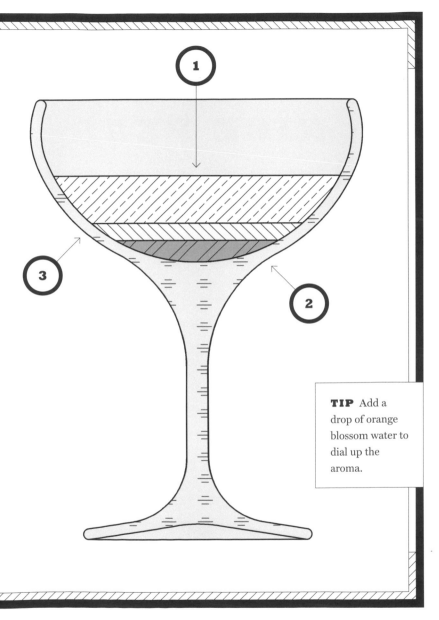

TIP Add a drop of orange blossom water to dial up the aroma.

NICE PEAR

There's nothing like a nice, ripe pear. This cocktail makes full use of this fact with freshly squeezed pear juice, a spicy note of ginger and a top-quality gin.

INGREDIENTS

1	pear juice, freshly squeezed	60 ml (2 oz)
2	premium gin	60 ml (2 oz)
3	homemade Spiced Brown Sugar Syrup (page 47)	15 ml (½ oz)
4	crystallised ginger, grated	to garnish
5	fresh mint sprig	to garnish

EQUIPMENT Shaker, strainer

METHOD Shake the wet ingredients over ice and strain into a coupe. Grate over a little crystallised ginger and add a sprig of mint to garnish.

GLASS TYPE:
COUPE

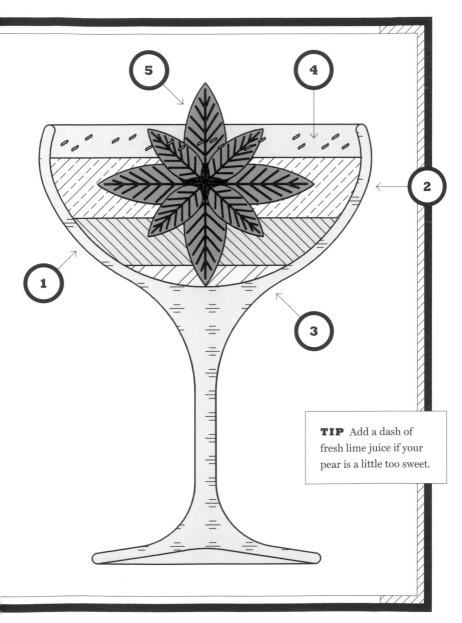

TIP Add a dash of fresh lime juice if your pear is a little too sweet.

GIN & JAM COCKTAIL

Think about it: jam is a splendid bedfellow for gin. It's a fruit-and-sugar combo that's perfect to bring in the sweet-and-sour notes that make up the perfect cocktail. Plus, there's something pleasingly dirty about stirring a spoonful of your favourite preserve into alcohol and sipping it over ice.

INGREDIENTS

1	gin	60 ml (2 oz)
2	lemon juice, freshly squeezed	30 ml (1 oz)
3	raspberry jam	2 tsp
4	homemade Simple Syrup (page 45)	15 ml (½ oz)
5	fresh mint sprig	to garnish

EQUIPMENT Shaker, strainer

METHOD Shake the gin, lemon juice, 1 teaspoon of jam and syrup over ice. Strain into a glass filled with crushed ice, stir in the second teaspoon of jam and garnish with a mint sprig. Cut out the Simple Syrup if you don't have a sweet tooth.

GLASS TYPE:
TUMBLER
OR HIGHBALL

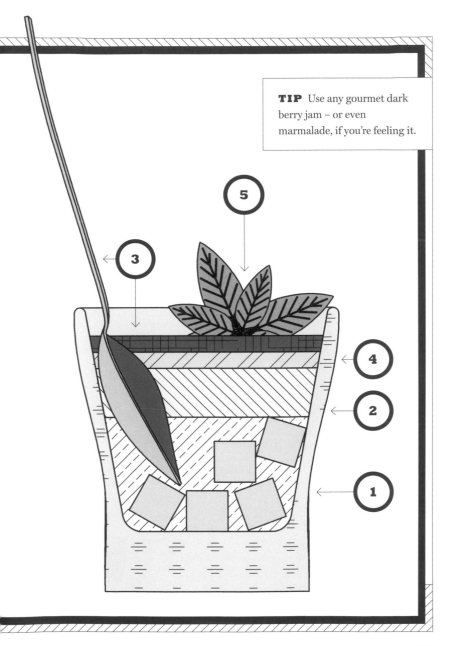

133

TIP Use any gourmet dark berry jam – or even marmalade, if you're feeling it.

THE SNOOP
(AKA GIN & JUICE)

Back in 1993, Snoop Dogg rapped about Gin & Juice on his debut album *Doggystyle,* and the drink formerly associated with grandmothers everywhere suddenly had its own gangsta swagger. It's potent and the cinnamon adds a little fire. Make sure the citrus juices are freshly squeezed.

SERVES 10–12

INGREDIENTS

1	lime juice, freshly squeezed	175 ml (6 oz)
2	homemade Cinnamon Syrup (page 49)	175 ml (6 oz)
3	gin	750 ml (25 oz)
4	cranberry juice	350 ml (12 oz)
5	pineapple juice	350 ml (12 oz)
6	orange juice, freshly squeezed	350 ml (12 oz)
7	orange slices	to garnish
8	lime slices	to garnish
9	pineapple chunks or slices	to garnish

EQUIPMENT Pitcher

METHOD Add the lime juice, cinnamon syrup and gin to the pitcher and stir well. Add the remaining wet ingredients over large ice cubes. Garnish with slices of fruit.

GLASS TYPE:
PITCHER
AND PAPER CUPS

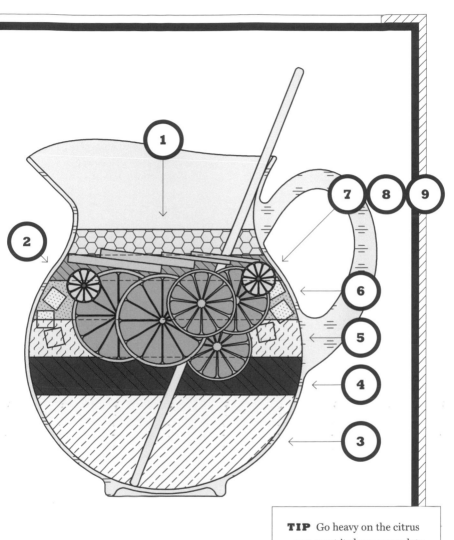

TIP Go heavy on the citrus – you want it sharp enough to knock your dentures out.

APEROL GIN PUNCH

This summery, Negroni-inspired punch uses fresh pink grapefruit juice and Italian soft and sweet herbal liqueur, Galliano, to give it an edge, with chilled Prosecco to make you go cross-eyed.

SERVES 10–12

INGREDIENTS

1	gin	1.25 litres (2¼ pints/5 cups)
2	Aperol	725 ml (1¼ pints/3 cups)
3	Galliano	250 ml (8¼ oz/1 cup)
4	lime juice, freshly squeezed	500 ml (17 oz/2 cups)
5	pink grapefruit juice, freshly squeezed	625 ml (1 pint/2½ cups)
6	orange bitters	splash
7	chilled Prosecco	to top up
8	thin orange slices	to garnish
9	thin lime slices	to garnish

EQUIPMENT Punch bowl or pitcher

METHOD Mix the ingredients in a punch bowl (with an ice block) or pitcher (with ice) and serve over ice-filled punch glasses or tumblers.

GLASS TYPE:
PUNCH GLASSES
OR TUMBLERS

137

HONEY BEAR GIN PUNCH

Bears love honey. And humans love gin. Why not combine the two in one powerful punch with Prosecco that will make everyone – hairy or not – super-happy. Does it taste 100 per cent delicious? Do bears sh*t in the woods?

SERVES 10–12

INGREDIENTS

1	gin	1.25 litres (2¼ pints)
2	homemade Honey Syrup (page 49)	250 ml (8½ oz)
3	lemon juice, freshly squeezed	250 ml (8½ oz)
4	Angostura bitters	splash
5	chilled Prosecco	to top up
6	fresh sage sprigs	to garnish
7	thin lemon slices	to garnish

EQUIPMENT Punch bowl or pitcher

METHOD Mix the ingredients in a punch bowl (with an ice block) or pitcher (with ice) and serve over ice-filled punch glasses or tumblers.

GLASS TYPE:
PUNCH GLASSES
OR TUMBLERS

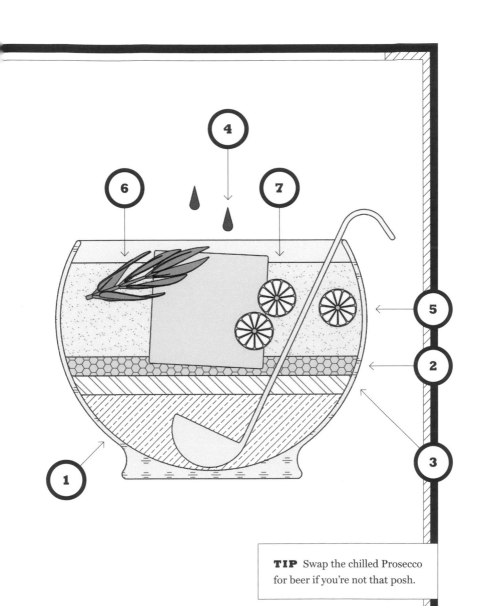

TIP Swap the chilled Prosecco for beer if you're not that posh.

DICKENS' HOT GIN PUNCH

It's not all about summer-quenching and dithering about with a cucumber: hot gin punch is the perfect winter warmer with a rich literary history. Here follows a recipe close to the gin punch that Charles Dickens' Mr Micawber gets tipsy on.

SERVES 10–12

INGREDIENTS

1	premium gin	750 ml (24 oz/3 cups)
2	Madeira wine	750 ml (24 oz/3 cups)
3	whole cloves	pinch
4	nutmeg, grated	pinch
5	ground cinnamon	generous pinch
6	homemade Spiced Brown Sugar Syrup (page 47)	dash
7	lemon juice, freshly squeezed	90 ml (3 oz)
8	lemon slices	to garnish
9	pineapple chunks	1 small pineapple
10	honey	4 tablespoons

EQUIPMENT Heavy-based saucepan

METHOD Add all the ingredients to a heavy-based saucepan and heat gently for around 30 minutes, adding a dash more honey or lemon to taste. The flavour intensifies the longer you let the punch simmer. Ladle into punch glasses – or pour it from a teapot if you're that way inclined.

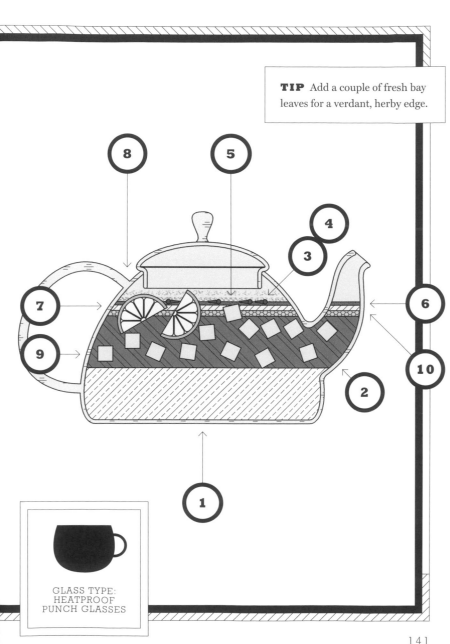

TIP Add a couple of fresh bay leaves for a verdant, herby edge.

8

5

4

3

7

9

6

10

2

1

GLASS TYPE:
HEATPROOF
PUNCH GLASSES

INDEX

ABOUT
DAN JONES

Perhaps the world's most prolific cocktail enjoyer, Dan Jones is a writer and editor living in London, having worked at a string of titles – from *i-D* magazine to *Time Out*. A self-professed homebody, he is well versed in the art of at-home drinking and loves to entertain, constantly 'researching' his cocktail craft and trying out new recipes. His favourite drink is a Dirty Martini. A really dirty one.